D0477407

SWEAT AND INSPIRATION

PIONEERS OF THE INDUSTRIAL AGE

MARTIN WORTH

SUTTON PUBLISHING

First published in the United Kingdom in 1999 by
Sutton Publishing Limited · Phoenix Mill
Thrupp · Stroud · Gloucestershire · GL5 2BU

Reprinted 1999

Copyright © Martin Worth, 1999

All rights reserved. No part of this publication may be reproduced, stored in a
retrieval system, or transmitted, in any form, or by any means, electronic,
mechanical, photocopying, recording or otherwise, without the prior permission
of the publisher and copyright holder.

Martin Worth has asserted the moral right to be identified as the author of this
work.

British Library Cataloguing in Publication Data
A catalogue record for this book is available from the British Library

ISBN 0 7509 1660 5

The title *Sweat and Inspiration* was first used for a BBC Radio 4 series about the
nineteenth-century engineers, also written by Martin Worth.

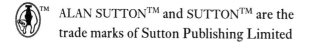

ALAN SUTTON™ and SUTTON™ are the
trade marks of Sutton Publishing Limited

Typeset in 11/15pt Ehrhardt.
Typesetting and origination by
Sutton Publishing Limited.
Printed in Great Britain by
Redwood Books Limited,
Trowbridge, Wiltshire.

Contents

List of Illustrations

Sources

Most of the illustrations are taken from long out-of-copyright published works. That of Leith in 1798 is from Cassell's *Old and New Edinburgh* by James Grant, 1829; the storm-driven ship from Falconer's *The Shipwreck*, 1808; and all the drawings of work on the Bell Rock lighthouse are from Robert Stevenson's *Account of the Bell Rock Lighthouse*, published in 1824. The drawings depicting the construction of the Thames tunnel can be found in *Memoir of the Life of Sir Marc Brunel* by Richard Beamish, who took an active part in the undertaking and wrote a vivid account of it in his book, published in 1862. Similarly, the line drawings related to the work of Trevithick can all be found in the two-volume biography of him written by his son Francis, which also contains the engraving by W. Holl of Trevithick's portrait and two others by W. Welch, the cottage at Penyponds and his version of Rowlandson's watercolour painting of the 'Catch-Me-Who-Can' locomotive on its circular track in Bloomsbury.

For other illustrations I am grateful to the following for their kind permission to let me reproduce them:

The Institution of Civil Engineers, for the portraits of the Brunels, the Stephensons, Joseph Locke, John Rennie and Thomas Telford. Also for the prints of Telford's Menai bridge and his design for the Clifton one, navvies building cuttings and embankments, work on the Thames tunnel, Forth Bridge and Crystal Palace, photographs of the attempted launch of the *Great Eastern*, and of Stephenson's bridge over the Tyne at Newcastle.

The Welsh Industrial & Maritime Museum, for their replica of Trevithick's Penydaren locomotive.

The Science Museum, Science and Society Picture Library, for Trevithick's model steam engine, the opening of the Liverpool–Manchester railway, and the steam road carriage.

The Post Office, all rights reserved, for the coaches at Elephant & Castle, London.

Angus Council, Cultural Services, for Robert Stevenson's map of Bell Rock and for the print of Arbroath in 1823.

The Library of the Religious Society of Friends in Britain for the portrait of Edward Pease.

Phil Green for his photo of the Bell Rock lighthouse today.

Crown copyright: Royal Commission on the Ancient and Historical Monuments Record of Wales for the aerial photograph of the Pont Cysyllte aqueduct.

John Binding Collection for Brunel's Royal Albert Bridge at Saltash.

The British Library, for *Illustrated London News* drawings of the Crystal Palace, the *Great Eastern*, and the completion of Brunel's Thames tunnel.

Elton Collection; Ironbridge Gorge Museum Trust, for their print of Stephenson's London–Birmingham railway crossing bridge at Bletchley.

Catherine Nasskau for the same scene today; to her too, for a modern LT train in Brunel's Thames tunnel, and the Tring cutting as it is today.

The History Collection in the Civil Engineering Department Library, Imperial College, for contemporary photographs of work on the Forth Bridge.

FURTHER ACKNOWLEDGEMENTS

For invaluable assistance with the text and research, I am particularly grateful to Mike Chrimes, Librarian of the Institution of Civil Engineers, and to Carol Arrowsmith of their Archives Department. Also to Quentin Stevenson, descendant of the lighthouse builder, Robert, who allowed me to quote from many of his great-great-grandfather's papers and letters, and to the Trustees of the National Library of Scotland, where they are lodged, for giving me access to them. Also to the Signal Tower Museum at Arbroath for prints and records related to the Bell Rock lighthouse, for much useful local history information and for indefatigable help from Margaret Thompson there and the Curator, Margaret King.

Prologue

On 8 August 1829, by the river Lackawaxen at Honesdale in Pennsylvania, an excited crowd stared amazed at the first steam locomotive they'd ever seen. It had the face of a lion embossed on the front of its boiler (though some said it looked more like a gigantic grasshopper) and had been built in England – at the Stourbridge works of John Rastrick – with the fanciful appearance given to it that had presumably been asked for by the American who had ordered it, Horatio Allen.

Allen had previously been employed by the Delaware and Hudson Canal Company which transported coal to their barges in wagons drawn by horses along a wooden tramway. It was to see if a locomotive could do this job more effectively that Allen had gone to England to check out the work in this field that was known to be going on there. He was so impressed by what he saw he gave orders for three locomotives to be shipped across the Atlantic at vast expense, the first to arrive being the one he had nicknamed the Stourbridge Lion.

That August morning, to cheers from the crowd and the booming of cannon in salute, Allen turned the throttle-valve, as he called it, and in his own words 'set off with considerable velocity, was soon out of hearing of cheers from the assembly present, and after two or three miles returned without accident, having thus made the first railroad trip by locomotive in the Western hemisphere.'

But it was a trip not ever made again by the Stourbridge Lion. Much too heavy for the wooden tramway, it was left abandoned where it stood, a fearsome-looking object that apparently scared children whenever they passed it, its parts stripped off one by one over the years by anyone who could find a use for them.

It had simply arrived too soon. Before any such locomotives could be put to good use, the great iron railroads that would open up the continent and enable this emergent nation – at that time barely fifty years old – to draw on its enormous untapped resources had yet to be built. It didn't take long. Ten years later over 3,000 miles of railroad had been laid and American engineers were fast catching up. But until then it was their pioneering colleagues in Britain who led the field.

On the continent of Europe the long drawn out Napoleonic wars had given most countries far more to worry about than how to raise their manufacturing capacity and build the infrastructure to serve it. Only Britain had been saved from bloodshed on her own land; those who died for their country had done so at sea or on foreign soil. So in the first half of the nineteenth century, with continental Europe in a state of political instability and the USA still finding its feet before rising to take over, it was Britain that had the best chance to exploit what we now call the Industrial Revolution and lay the foundations for the kind of world most of us live in today.

Whether we like our present day environment or not, it was largely brought into being by a small group of British engineers who rarely get the acknowledgment due to them, except from those who have made a special study of their work, or follow the profession they created. Most people anywhere in the developed world just take for granted their man-made surroundings, and never spare a thought for how they came to be there. In the Americas, in Africa, India, Australia, Asia and all over Europe, people still travel today on the very roads and railways, through tunnels and cuttings, over bridges and embankments, that were built so long ago by men with scant scientific knowledge to rely on, no machinery and no source of energy other than that of horses and the muscle power of labourers.

Yet within the space of no more than two generations it was just such men who turned the pastoral Britain of the early 1800s into the largely urbanised country it has since become and opened the way for all other countries to do the same.

Biographies of early nineteenth-century engineers, and other books assessing their work, have largely been written for people with a special interest in the subject, with emphasis on their extraordinary technical achievements. So relatively few have heard the story as a whole – not as a detailed history of civil engineering, but as a human saga recounting the struggles of some half dozen individuals who hardly even realised at the time what their work would lead to.

They were men of very different characters and backgrounds. None of them were formally trained as engineers; it was not a profession even recognised when they began to change the face of the world. Each had his own particular strengths and weaknesses as a human being, and all were in one way or another affected by the women in their lives. And they lived in a world where, unlike their counterparts today, they mostly depended on none but themselves to get what they wanted.

They needed no imports from foreign suppliers. They weren't at the mercy of government economic policies, and rarely even wanted help from government funds. When Isambard Brunel was surveying his route for the Great Western Railway, he was confident his company could not only acquire all the land it needed, but build the embankments, tunnel through the hills, bridge the rivers, forge the rails and make the locomotives on money raised entirely by a group of businessmen in Bristol. And Robert Stephenson operated in just the same way. As they walked or rode about the countryside surveying their routes, they had no planning authorities to contend with and no accountants from Head Office breathing down their necks. They negotiated for everything as occasion arose, whether with contractors, landowners or labourers, and had to be as skilful businessmen as they were engineers.

So no wonder they got things done so quickly. In the 1840s a three-mile tunnel was driven through the Pennines in less time than it took for a similar tunnel to be bored through the same hill by machinery in the 1950s. And when Daniel Gooch was asked by Brunel to make a super express locomotive he'd designed to fight off a challenge from Stephenson, the completed engine with every part specially made for it steamed out of the sheds at Swindon just two months later.

Most people today are not very interested in engineering since it smacks of technical and scientific processes they know little about. But the basic knowledge of the men who started it all – from which everything they created directly derived – is something each one of us can understand. We may not know exactly how electricity works, or grasp the complexities of the internal combustion engine. But neither of these sources of power and the uses derived from them was known to the pioneer engineers either. They simply knew that the vast quantities of iron ore which lay in profusion beneath their hills and valleys could be smelted in furnaces burning coal, which was equally plentiful, till it was sufficiently molten to be fashioned into any shape or size their gigantic imaginations conceived of – and that such shapes could be made to move by the colossal power of a steam engine. And the simple principle of a steam engine is something we can all understand. Boil water in a saucepan and all can see that any lid on top of it will lift.

That's all you need to know to appreciate the work of the early nineteenth-century engineers. For an assessment of what each achieved, there are plenty of brilliant biographies available to which due acknowledgement for their help with this book is made in the bibliography. But they all lived at roughly the same time, their lives and work interweaving with each other's to make up the unfolding story of how the industrialised world we see around us today first came into being.

It had its origins in the multifarious scientific developments that followed from the invention of the steam engine in the eighteenth century. But it was in the early 1800s, when the nations of Europe were at war and America had only just begun to get going as a free independent country, that the story began to make the impact from which the world was never to recover.

CHAPTER ONE

Danger at Sea

It had terrorised seamen for centuries. It was a quarter of a mile long and some eighty yards across, but it was only twice a day, for an hour either side of low tide, that it ever revealed itself. Mostly it lurked undetected beneath deceptively calm water.

In the eighteenth century navigators making south down the coast of Scotland towards the Firth of Forth could tell from landmarks and their charts in what direction lay the dangerous Inchcape reef, and roughly how far off it was. But they never knew exactly where the wind would blow them. So, once out of sight of land and in the vicinity of the reef, it was impossible to tell just how close to danger they were.

Noticing around them restless breakers, or even in calm weather unexpected ripples on the surface, a ship's Master might fear that already the rock is right underneath them. He calls for soundings. Maybe fourteen fathoms is reported, even twelve, anxiety now turning to alarm. But presently the line reads eighteen, followed quickly by twenty, twenty-two, twenty-four! With the breakers left behind and the water around them now relatively calm, all hands are relieved that they seem to have passed over safely.

But just as they give thanks, the deck judders to the sound of a searing crunch beneath them as the teeth of the unseen monster tear away their keel. That the water immediately surrounding the rock is so much deeper than that farther off was known only to those who never lived to warn anyone else.

From Arbroath, on the Scottish coast between Dundee and Montrose, the Inchcape rock stands eleven miles out to sea and so right in the middle of the north-east approach to the Firth of Forth. Such was the terror it inspired that in rough weather ships would often prefer to ride it out at sea than seek the shelter of the Firth and risk a meeting with its vicious underwater sentinel.

As far back as the Middle Ages it had caused so many wrecks that in 1394, so the story goes, the Abbot of Aberbrothock, as Arbroath was called then, had taken action. He is said to have had a large bronze bell cast, and after landing on the rock with his monks during the very short time it was exposed to the air had managed to set it up above the highest tide. He ingeniously fixed it so it would be swayed to and fro by the waves and continually ring out its warning to all within earshot. But it seems there was a pirate known as Ralph the Rover who reckoned a big bronze bell would be a valuable addition to his booty. So he made off with it one night. One year later, writes the scribe who recounted this story, the Rover and his ship found themselves again in these waters and at night in very rough weather. But with no bell now to warn them of their peril, the rock struck back – and down went the pirate 'to perish with his ship and goods in the righteous judgment of God.'

By the 1790s the Bell Rock, as the reef was now called, was bringing increasing havoc to shipping. With the expansion of trade with Scandinavia and the Baltic, ships were constantly crossing the North Sea to and from the Scottish and north-east English ports. Often on their approach to these shores the Bell Rock reef stood right in their path.

In December 1799 a gale got up in the North Sea that raged from Yarmouth to the Shetlands. Ships at rest in the roads at east coast ports were driven off their moorings; others at sea were blown to well beyond Aberdeen. Had it not been for the danger from the hidden Bell Rock, many would have sought the safety of the Firth of Forth. Two did and suffered the consequences on the rock. Others, terrified of what might be in store for them there, stayed out at sea – only to find themselves blown to where the gale turned out to be even worse. In one cove alone the wreckage of seven separate boats was washed up with no survivors. It was reported in Edinburgh that over the three days the gale was blowing more than sixty ships went down.

There had long been a demand for some kind of light on the Bell Rock. Until the Northern Lighthouse Board (NLB) was formed in 1786, whatever lights there were on dangerous coasts in Scotland consisted of no more than open fires, kept alight by the landowners who claimed dues at the nearest port from the ships that benefited from them. But soon the NLB was building proper lighthouses wherever it could, and in 1793 was urged by an Admiral to build one on Bell Rock which 'lay in the most dangerous situation possible'. He stressed the good it would bring to the traders of Scotland and would have added the Royal Navy too, had he known that ten years later in 1803 – at a time when all warships were sorely needed for the fight against Napoleon at sea – the frigate HMS *York* was to hit the rock in heavy seas, drift off and subsequently go down with her 64 guns and 491 men.

That a light was needed on Bell Rock was as obvious to the Board's Commissioners as to anyone else. But to build eleven miles out at sea? On something that for twenty out of every twenty-four hours was totally submerged? Nevertheless, they were open to practicable ideas from any quarter and after the great storm of 1799 advertised the fact.

And they already employed a young man for whom building a lighthouse on the Bell Rock had been his ambition for the last six years.

His name was Robert Stevenson. An only child whose father had died when Robert was two, he had been brought up in Edinburgh by his widowed mother who hoped he would one day enter the Ministry. She was a deeply committed Christian – not Church of Scotland, but a Baptist – and it was at their local Baptist church that she and her son got to know Thomas Smith.

Smith was an energetic, self-employed lighting engineer with his own workshop where he designed and manufactured oil lamps. They gave out so much radiance that the architects of the splendid new Georgian houses being built for the rapidly expanding city were everywhere engaging him to provide such lighting for their clients. The success of Smith's lamps depended on his use of a curved reflector behind a glass-enclosed wick that made the light shine out like a beam. Since oil lamps were already used in this way in English lighthouses, it wasn't long before Smith was designing such lights for the Northern Lighthouse Board, and very soon the lighthouses themselves. With the City Fathers of Edinburgh now asking him to provide street lighting for the entire city (which meant the manufacture and installation of 594 lamps), Thomas was so busy he hardly spent a day at home.

When Jean Stevenson first met him, he was married with three young daughters and a son. But one of his daughters died when she was three – to be replaced in the family almost at once by another son. Within a year this boy died too, followed shortly by the death of his exhausted mother. Distressed but unbowed, Smith immediately found a second wife who was happy to bring up his family.

By now he had got to know Jean and her son. He was so impressed by the boy he persuaded his mother he was more cut out for engineering than the Church and, to Robert's delight, made him his apprentice. Having lost two children of his own in infancy, he seems to have taken as much a paternal as a professional interest in the fourteen-year-old Robert Stevenson, so fit, healthy, intelligent and industrious. He saw to his education – very soon would send him to Edinburgh University – and clearly regarded him as one of the family.

Early in 1791 his second wife had a child of her own, another girl. But she died within days of her birth. Her mother was so distressed that in her weak post-natal state she was taken seriously ill and died herself. And this was just at the time that Thomas Smith was about to set off on an urgent visit to the lighthouses, having heard they were running out of oil. What could he do? Two girls under twelve and an eight-year-old son? Jean Stevenson promised to take care of them for him, and moved in with Robert while he was away. He returned four months later and almost at once, in September 1791, he asked her to marry him and she happily accepted.

From now on, Robert was to become a surrogate son to Thomas Smith who, even when Robert had become very much his own man some twelve years later, was proudly signing himself as 'your ever affectionate father'. And doubtless Robert, who had never known his real father at all, was happy to see him in that way too.

From Thomas he learnt so much that, whenever Smith was unavailable for lighthouse work due to his increasing commitments in Edinburgh, Robert was able to take his place. At twenty-two he had already supervised the completion of a lighthouse on the river Clyde, and was put in charge of building two more. Soon he had taken over from Thomas the annual inspection of all the Board's lights and by 1797, though still studying in the winter at Edinburgh University, was well on the way to being appointed their official engineer.

In that year his mother, married to Smith for five years now and in her mid-forties, brought another addition to his family by bearing him a daughter. They named her Elizabeth after Thomas's beloved first wife. Nicknamed Betsy, she was doted on by her parents.

Two years later, as if to bring the two families even closer, Robert himself married the eldest Smith girl, Jeannie.

Her real name was Jean, the same as Robert's mother, so to avoid confusion in the Smith household she was either called Jane or Jeannie. Having lived with her as his sister for the preceding eight years, did Robert suddenly discover at twenty-seven he had feelings for her not brotherly at all? If so, he would certainly have repressed them and concentrated hard on his work. But if he took after his mother in keeping his feelings to himself, Jeannie had no hesitation in showing hers and in that respect inherited her father's nature as much as Robert inherited his mother's.

A tall woman with patrician features – a straight Roman nose and high forehead – Jeannie was just as devout a Christian as Robert's mother (who had, after all,

Edinburgh's port at Leith in 1798, from which Thomas Smith and Robert Stevenson set sail on their visits to the lighthouses. Within twenty-five years steam tugs and mechanised cranes had turned such harbours into industrialised docks.

A miniature portrait of young Robert Stevenson, whose battle with nature on a submerged rock in the North Sea exemplified the spirit of all the pioneering engineers.

The forces of nature, which could wreak such havoc to shipping in the North Sea, were by then being gradually tamed.

brought her up) and, along with her younger sister Janet, was always active in doing good works among the poor. After the wedding – which took place at the Baptist church where the two families had first met – the couple continued to live at their parents' home in Baxters Place where Jean senior ruled as matriarch.

It was very much the women who dominated the household. Not only were the men away so much on business – between May and October Robert was away most of the time on his annual inspection of the lighthouses – but even when at home both he and his father-in-law were regularly out on training exercises with the city's militia, the Grenadier Volunteers. Formed to help put down any sedition that might come in the wake of the French Revolution, the Volunteers liked to think, as they drilled in their colourful uniforms, that Buonaparte would be in for a very nasty surprise if he should ever be spotted sailing up the Firth with an invading army. Smith so hated the French that many years later in his old age he would get out a collection of toy tin soldiers and re-enact the Napoleonic wars with anyone willing to play the enemy and agree to be utterly destroyed. There was serious trouble in the family home if somehow or other his opponent managed to win.

In his prime, however, the affluent way of life that the family enjoyed, thanks to his success as lamp designer, manufacturer, engineer and businessman, was not something the women in his household altogether approved of. It was both his wife's and his daughter's opinion that to build up treasure in Heaven was more important than to gather it on earth. The fact that Jeannie seems to have had fairly extravagant tastes in clothes, having wanted for nothing from her successful father all her life, did not deter her from making Robert feel that, in the eyes of the Lord, it was his spiritual not his material achievements that mattered most.

Not surprisingly, Jeannie was known to everyone as kind to a fault. After the death of one of her children, a former nursemaid wrote her a letter of condolence – adding she was herself to be pitied too, being so unhappy in her job and sure Mrs Stevenson could find her a better one. On one occasion, when her husband complained about a tough joint of beef he was carving, Jeannie told him that whether it was the fault of their cook or the butcher both were devout Christians; they had little or nothing put by to live on and so deserved their patronage, however poor their skills. The midwives who delivered her babies were chosen not for their proficiency but according to how much they needed the money.

Robert, of course, expected value for money at all times. And he was a stickler for tidiness, punctuality and order. On his voyages to inspect the lighthouses, he mercilessly berated any keeper who did not polish the furniture in his living quarters. Even though he knew there was no one to see the result but the keeper himself, it was his opinion that such a man might prove equally lackadaisical in maintaining the light. That there were ships at sea totally dependent on the keeper's absolute reliability was something Stevenson never failed to instil.

On all his inspection voyages, sailing north from the Firth, Robert's ship had had to pass the Bell Rock; and he was as nervous as anyone else when they crossed its latitude at high tide. He had long wanted to land on it to see what kind of lighthouse might be possible. After the storm of 1799 he was determined to do so. So as soon as the winter was over, in April 1800, he set off with a resolute crew. But they were driven back by a storm. On another occasion the sea was so bad that even at low tide there were breakers smashing over it. It wasn't till October, when he'd almost given up hope of managing it before the winter set in again, that at last he succeeded.

By now he had made a model of what he thought might be possible on this ferocious bit of land, so jealously guarded by the sea. It stood on six cast-iron pillars driven deep into the rock which would break up the attacking waves and disperse their force around them rather than against them. Given the difficulties of working at all on such a dangerous site so far from land, the boring of holes to take the pillars would be the only foundation work required; and whatever the structure they had to support could be mostly prefabricated. The Commissioners, on being shown Robert's plan and model, reckoned it might not prove too expensive either.

Wanting all the professional advice he could muster, Robert persuaded James Haldane, who taught him architectural drawing at university, to come with him. Having been promised the loan of a Customs yacht at Elie to take them, they got there to learn it had suddenly been put in for repairs. With the tides only right for them over the next few days, time was running out. Some fishermen they asked made it clear that not even for money would they sail anywhere near the Bell Rock. At last at Broughty Ferry, birthplace as it happened of Thomas Smith, they found some boatmen who visited the rock often – to scavenge for anything of value that the latest wrecks had left on it. They knew the inshore waters well, and the best place to land.

They arrived just when the tide was at its lowest. The sun was shining, the sea calm and as Robert stepped ashore, to set foot at last on this monster he hoped to tame for ever, he had precisely two hours to get all the information he needed.

It didn't take him long to realise that his plan to build on cast-iron pillars was out of the question. As he later told Smith, 'I had no sooner landed than I saw my pillars tumble like the baseless fabric of a dream!' Even in such tranquil weather, the sea was attacking and retreating angrily through narrow fissures, swirling impatiently around inlets and sweeping up the sides of the highest part of the rock that stood, even at low tide, only seven ft at most above the surface. It was easy to imagine the effect of waves in weather only moderately rough: to unload supplies a boat would have to come in close and be in danger of being smashed to bits against the iron pillars. And in Haldane's opinion cast iron was treacherous anyway, always liable to snap under stress without warning.

Robert knew that under the water the rock extended for some 1,200 ft, but the only part of it ever exposed was what they were surveying now. They calculated it at about 240 ft long by 120 across at its widest. Sloping down towards the northern end, its seaweed and jagged rocks made it almost impossible to stay upright when walking. Even the boatmen, who had been here often, were having difficulty. They staggered about, peering closely into the pools left by the tide and dredging up anything they thought worth having.

Robert left them to it as he set about making a sketch map. But all too soon the little island began to grow rapidly smaller as the tide came jealously in to hide it again. The men called them to get into the dinghy, and in it Robert noticed their trophies, a ship's kedge anchor, part of a galley stove, a bayonet, a brooch, a cooking pot, a cannon ball and a silver shoe buckle. He argued that with such finds they should reduce the price they had charged for bringing him here. But the men were not having that. One guinea per man is what they agreed, and one for the boat. It doesn't say much for Robert that he tried to beat them down, even less that, on his own admission many years later, he claimed some of their salvage findings for himself. No employer ever did more for the welfare of his men as events will show; but when it came to laying out money, no one ever drove harder bargains.

Money may well have been on his mind just then, having realised, as he sailed back to the mainland with Haldane that October afternoon, that what he was now going to propose to mark the rock would cost very much more than a structure on iron pillars.

Nothing less would do, he thought, than a massive tower some 90 ft high, with sides soaring up in a parabolic curve from a very wide base and foundations dug deep into the rock. Later he calculated that the stone used would weigh 2,620 tons, compared with the mere 200 tons of his cast-iron pillar proposal. He argued from this not that such a colossal weight would, therefore, be beyond the skill of man to raise on such a hostile and remote site, but simply that it would then prove to be so much stronger and more lasting.

Just how he was to build it he had at that time no idea. But it never crossed his mind it might not be possible to build it at all. If you have never even heard of electricity, or the internal combustion engine, or imagined that steam power could ever have a future beyond the factory, if cranes to you are little more than manually powered hoists, if anemometers or any other device to measure the velocity and power of wind and wave are beyond the limits of even the most fanciful imagination, if all the aids without which no such feat today would even be contemplated are not known even to exist, then of course you don't miss them. What is remarkable is that men like Stevenson had as grand a vision as any engineer could have today and, without any of the technology his modern counterpart depends on, just as much confidence in turning the dream into reality.

The Lighthouse Board, however, was more sceptical. Admittedly, John Smeaton had built the renowned Eddystone lighthouse off Plymouth which was even further out to sea. But it was not on a rock only ever visible for two hours each tide, and never the same two hours at that. Nevertheless, in view of the clamour for action that the gales of 1799 had whipped up, they did at least do something. They applied for an Act of Parliament that would allow them not just to build a lighthouse but to pay for it out of dues charged to shipping. Accordingly, in 1801, one of their number, a Commissioner who was himself the Lord Advocate and Member of Parliament for Edinburgh, promoted a Bill at Westminster.

It was thrown out, not by the Commons, but by the Lords who complained that to charge light dues at ports all along the east coast from every ship that crossed the latitude of the Bell Rock was extortionate. They proposed so many amendments that the Lord Advocate withdrew the Bill.

At least its rejection stiffened the resolve of the NLB. They urged traders and businessmen in Scotland to write to them in support of a lighthouse. And following their announcement that any practicable ideas for marking the position of the rock would be welcome, they received one from a certain Captain Brodie, RN, and his partner, Mr Coupar, an ironmaster in Leith. It recommended a structure on four cast-iron legs – very like the one which Robert had originally proposed but which he had now shown to be totally unseaworthy.

The Board was not impressed though they could see it would be a whole lot cheaper than what Robert had proposed. And they could hardly turn it down altogether on being told its sponsors would erect, at their own expense, temporary

John Smeaton, regarded as the father of civil engineering.

Smeaton's design for the Eddystone lighthouse off Plymouth, which pioneered the use of dovetailed interlocking stones for extra strength and became the role model for Stevenson's tower on Bell Rock.

wooden beacons to stand above the highest tide till their lighthouse was completed.

The first such beacon was almost at once washed away; so was the next, and the third, erected in July 1803, though strong enough to make it through the autumn, had gone for good by December. Though doubtless irritated by the attention the Board was giving these amateurs, Robert was far too professional to make an issue of it. He simply carried on with his other work – which included erecting a beacon light in the Orkneys and a full-scale lighthouse on Inchkeith in the Firth of Forth. He also made a long voyage through the Irish Sea to visit all the lighthouses from St Bee's in Cumberland to the Wolf Rock in the Isles of Scilly.

Later he set off again, by land this time, to visit fourteen more. It was a journey of 2,500 miles that took him from the Humber and Cromer in the east of England down to Portland and Plymouth in the south. Here he made a very close study of the lighthouse he had based his own on – the revered Eddystone, built on a rock off Plymouth by John Smeaton in 1759.

Smeaton had now been dead for seven years. But it was he who can be said to have founded the profession of Civil Engineering, having formed the Society of Civil Engineers at a London tavern in 1771. Although canals had long since been cutting into the countryside by then, the men who built them did not consider they belonged to a specific profession. But while Robert Stevenson had been growing up as a child in Edinburgh, there were other Scotsmen among his elders taking a very broad look at the scene around them and laying the foundations for the infrastructure of the very different world we know today.

One such was John Rennie. He revered Smeaton as the father of civil engineering and possibly saw himself as the man most fitted to carry it on. By 1800 he had become the most celebrated civil engineer in Great Britain. Such was his reputation that Robert, before submitting to the Board his plans and model of the stone lighthouse he wanted to build, got Rennie to approve them. But even the great Rennie's backing did not at first count for anything with the Commissioners.

They were still at that time considering the Brodie/Coupar proposal. When they finally decided to reject it, they thanked the two men for their trouble and offered to pay their expenses. They were presented with a bill for several thousand pounds, being the amount they claimed would have accrued to them in royalties from shipping dues, had their lighthouse been built. The Board called their bluff, and they settled for £400.

But still the Board was reluctant to endorse their own engineer's proposal. They just didn't think it was practicable. Robert told them bitterly that if he had the money he'd put up 10 or 15 ft of the building at his own expense to convince them 'there is not the difficulty imagined'. Turning to Rennie, the Commissioners asked if he really did think such a lighthouse was the answer. Rennie went to check it out himself and afterwards reported that 'to mark the situation of this dangerous and frightful rock, nothing in my opinion will do except a stone lighthouse such as Mr Stevenson has proposed'.

Robert was delighted to have his support, and overjoyed to be told that in consequence the Board would now back his lighthouse all the way.

There was one proviso, however. The Board were so impressed by the great Rennie's approval that they decided to appoint him as Chief Engineer – with Robert to act merely as his assistant.

CHAPTER TWO

Smoke on the Road

John Rennie was six foot four, an enormous height in those days. Able to look down on everyone he met, he exuded an air of lofty self-importance that grew more and more marked the more successful he became.

In 1804 he had every reason to be pleased with himself. Everyone was after his services – to build a canal from Saltcoats to Glasgow, another from Portsmouth to London, to reconstruct Chichester Harbour and extend Southampton Docks, to engineer a scheme to drain the Fens, and another to flood the valley of the River Lea in the event of invasion by the French. He had built numerous bridges, and had recently been asked to design one to cross the Menai Straits. He had built the new Royal Mint in London, cornmills in Spain and harbour works at Cadiz, and was about to fulfil his biggest contract, the construction of the London Docks.

He was a farmer's son from East Linton, about twenty miles from Edinburgh. One of a large family, at the age of six he took himself so seriously he would never play with other children and even complained about the noise they made. Fascinated by machinery, he got himself apprenticed to the millwright Andrew Meikle and later, at his own request, went to Dunbar High School where he won all the prizes and became Head Boy. At nineteen he not only set up himself as a millwright but found the time also to study at Edinburgh University. Three years later, with the money made from his business, he set off for England with an introduction to another Scot, the celebrated James Watt, inventor of steam engines, who in Birmingham with his partner, Matthew Boulton, was supplying engines to factories and mills all over the country.

In London, a huge milling concern on the south bank of the Thames near Blackfriars Bridge had contracted with Boulton & Watt to mechanise their works. Appreciating Rennie's skill as a millwright and the understanding he had shown of the firm's engines, the partners sent him to London to carry out the contract. Rennie made such a success of it he was soon inviting the cream of London society to come and look at it all. This annoyed Watt. Always paranoiac about

John Rennie, from the portrait by Henry Raeburn.

anyone looking at his engines in case they tried to copy them, he protested that though Rennie was doubtless just indulging his vanity he would find that 'dukes and lords and noble peers will not be his best customers'.

But Rennie knew better. By assiduously cultivating the rich and influential, he obtained the most lucrative contracts. Proudly he wrote to his brother in Scotland that recently the Earl of Hopetoun no less had 'shaken me by the hand and invited me to visit him at his house in Albemarle Street.' Soon he made the acquaintance of the Prime Minister, William Pitt, who would often, so he liked to confide, drop in to see him at his home in Stamford Street on the south side of the river when wearied by affairs of state in Downing Street.

In 1788 he got engaged to be married, gleefully pointing out in a letter to his brother how rich the lady was. Apart from the handsome dowry she would bring him, he made no mention of any other qualities in her at all. But she must have got wise to him, for shortly afterwards he married someone else altogether – by whom he had several children including two sons who later followed so closely in their father's footsteps that they not only became engineers but as much figures of the establishment as he had ever been.

From a historical perspective it could be said that Rennie's cultivation of those who mattered most in contemporary society is at least as important as his engineering achievements. In 1800 England was still outwardly a green and pleasant land. The countryside stirred to the sound of the post horn from the passing stagecoach and, in the Quantock hills of Somerset, Wordsworth and Coleridge had composed their *Lyrical Ballads* and launched the great flood of romantic poetry. In the cities Beau Brummel was showing aristocrats how to dress, while soon John Nash would be building his elegant crescents and terraces. In such society it took a man like Rennie to raise the status of engineers above that of mere mechanics. Immensely proud of his profession, he made the aristocracy see that as an engineer he deserved at least as much respect as architects and men of letters. This was not a conscious, proselytising mission – simply the side-effect of his inordinate ego and commanding personality, towering as he did over everyone he met, with his mass of auburn hair and what has been referred to as his majestic head.

Many of the projects for which his professional advice was urgently sought, and handsomely paid for, never came to fruition at all. His plan to cross the Menai Straits with a 450 ft span iron bridge a hundred ft above the water was the result of a survey made by his assistant. It was never built. Nor was the bridge he proposed to cross the Don at Aberdeen, despite the four different designs he put forward. Nor were several canals he surveyed. But what of it? Rennie exuded such confidence in the transforming power of civil engineering, he had industrialists as excited as he was by all that could be done to wake up sleepy old pastoral Britain.

He was not one to get his hands dirty. He was making a big enough contribution without having to descend to such menial levels. So when appointed Chief Engineer to erect a lighthouse on Bell Rock, he informed the Commissioners:

> Mr Stevenson, to whose merit I am happy to bear ample testimony, has made a model of a lighthouse nearly resembling that of the Eddystone in which he has proposed various ingenious methods of constructing it to facilitate operations. But after considering these in the fullest manner and comparing them with the way Mr Smeaton's lighthouse was built, there is undoubted proof of the stability of the Eddystone so I am inclined to give that the preference. Considering it in this light, it will be unnecessary for me to accompany this report with the design of such a lighthouse. It will be time enough to make such a design when the Commissioners are in a situation to give orders for its erection, when I have no doubt Mr Stevenson will furnish me with much valuable matter towards the perfecting of it.

He had never built a lighthouse in his life. Robert Stevenson by now had built five, though all were on relatively accessible sites and not required to stand up to the onslaught of wind and wave to be faced by anything on a rock at sea. Because only the Eddystone had been built for comparable conditions and magnificently survived, it was natural for both engineers to consider closely what Smeaton had done to achieve this stability. His success was due largely to the way the stones had been laid, not simply on top of one other as even great castles had been built in the past, but shaped to interlock the way joints in wood are dovetailed by cabinet makers. Since Smeaton had made such a success of this method, it was understandable that Rennie should want this young engineer to follow him exactly. But he could see for himself that he could never improve on Robert's design and clearly had no serious intention of trying to do so, whatever he said to the Commissioners. He just wanted to be sure that, when it was built, he himself would get a very big share of the credit for it.

However bitter at heart Robert must surely have been at Rennie being placed over him, he had been far too properly brought up to show any resentment, and anyway knew very well that, if a Bill was to be put before Parliament again, it was far more likely to succeed with Rennie's name attached to it than his own.

To make sure, he went to London with a member of the NLB to meet up with Rennie and together lobby government officials – especially at the Treasury where at least half the money would come from. They also called on the Admiralty which had previously shown no interest at all; now, since the loss of the *York* on the rock, it was much more sympathetic. But it was Sir Joseph Banks, the botanist-explorer, now Vice-President of the Board of Trade, who drummed up most support in Whitehall. He had sailed along the Forfarshire coast himself and knew the danger from the rock at first hand.

After passing its First Reading, the Bill was referred to a parliamentary committee which closely examined both Stevenson and Rennie and clearly appreciated which of the two was the real designer of the lighthouse and would certainly be building it. Since the aim of the Bill was to allow the NLB to borrow half the money from the Treasury and raise the rest from the private sector, the estimated cost was critical. Robert declared it to be £42,685 8s. Not to be outdone by this absurdly precise computation, Rennie estimated 'from my own experience of works in the sea that the expense will amount to £41,843 15s.'

This time the Bill met no opposition from the Lords and on 6 July 1806 it received the Royal Assent. Robert was back in Scotland by then, happy in the knowledge that at last he had the chance to make his dream come true. But he was apprehensive. As he said in a letter to a friend, 'Although I have bestirred myself in this business for eight or ten years, yet now when the matter seems at hand I look forward with grave anxiety to the dangers and numberless difficulties which must be struggled with by all engaged in this work.'

He was little enough at home at the best of times, but from now on his wife would see even less of him. About eighteen months after their marriage, Jeannie had given birth to their first child, a girl, and eighteen months later another they called Janet. Then the following year, June 1803, twins were born, Thomas and

Elizabeth. Robert, away at the time, was delighted by 'the happy news of my now much increased family', telling Smith that he is sure his wife 'is in great spirits with such a prospect' and praying that 'God who disposes all things will perfect her recovery and spare us for a blessing to one another'. But in the same letter he is sorry to have heard that Betsy, his sister Elizabeth that his mother bore Thomas Smith, is still 'so weakly', commenting that 'we are indeed very uncertain of the events of this life . . . My mother must at this time be very distressed and require all our sympathy.'

Betsy, aged seven, died a few weeks later. Presumably Robert did more than just send his condolences through Thomas Smith, but one cannot be sure from this letter if he wrote even to his wife to congratulate her on the birth of the twins. Shy about expressing his feelings, even when safely wrapped in moral sentiments, he was a man's man who probably felt more at ease with his surrogate father Thomas than with the wife he loved.

At Baxters Place, a capacious house off Leith Walk, the Stevensons had one part, the Smiths another. The women ruled both. In one, Robert's wife was bringing up her three daughters and young son, assisted by a nursemaid; in the other, in 1806, was her 22-year-old sister, Janet, and Robert's mother. By then Thomas's son James was now twenty-three, and with Robert now exclusively committed to the Lighthouse Board and the Bell Rock project, it was James who took his place in the family lighting firm. Whether Thomas had the same confidence in his son as he did in Robert is, however, open to question.

That summer Robert had again made his annual inspection tour of the lighthouses and at some time, probably on his way back, had visited Arbroath – to tell the Town Council it would be here, as the port most contiguous, as he put it, to the rock, that he intended to make his base for the building of the lighthouse. So the immense preparations began.

Rennie, of course, stayed in London. This is where he lived, and with his London docks now nearing completion he had to be available if needed on the site. This is not to say he skimped his responsibilities to the NLB as Chief Engineer on their new lighthouse. When visiting Edinburgh in December he attended two of their meetings and wrote constantly to Robert with advice on how to proceed.

But besides the London docks – and he had now been asked to prepare schemes for the docks at Hull, Peterhead, Ramsgate and Fraserburgh – he had also received a commission from the Admiralty to assess the progress made in the mechanisation of the Royal Dockyards. It would be two years before he completed this assignment

– after all, he had so much else to do as well – but it's clear from his Report of 1808 he had made a close study of the machinery in use at Portsmouth.

The fact that for some time now ships' blocks – those pulleys whereby seamen can raise and lower sails – had been mass-produced on a mechanised assembly line at the Portsmouth Dockyard must surely have come to his attention. Till 1803 they had been virtually made by hand. But a foreign engineer, a Frenchman who'd been living in New York, had patented machinery which so impressed the Admiralty they had signed him up to instal it. There is, however, no record that John Rennie met the man in question – one Marc Brunel who, in 1806, had just become the very proud father of a son he named Isambard.

Rennie was much too puffed up with his own importance to have given any more than the time of day to some excitable French engineer. But had he known that Marc Brunel was a close friend of the former First Lord of the Admiralty, Earl Spencer, he might have felt differently. As it was, he was no more interested in the work of Marc Brunel than in that of an engineer at that time trying to bore a tunnel under the Thames. He had been consulted on this project himself once and thought the idea so impracticable as to be hardly worth consideration. It did not surprise him at all that they were having such problems with it.

What did surprise him was to hear in 1807 whom the company had now appointed to take over. He was not what today we would call a civil engineer at all, but the inventor of steam engines that had become rivals to James Watt's and for that reason alone not approved of by Rennie – a Cornishman called Richard Trevithick.

Trevithick was also tall. And so strong he thought nothing of slinging a blacksmith's mandril weighing half a ton over his shoulder or nonchalantly tossing a sledge-hammer across the roof of a building. Once after a formal dinner, when everyone was happily drunk – and Trevithick could drink anyone under the table – he agreed to a friendly wrestling bout with someone, turned him upside down and planted his footsteps on the ceiling. It was done with the greatest good humour, but since he was also known to have a very quick temper it was hardly surprising that few risked crossing him on matters he cared about.

Nicknamed the Cornish Giant, he was just one year older than Robert Stevenson, the only son of an engine manager at a mining company. Spoilt by his mother, he did much as he liked as a child and was regarded at school as lazy and obstinate. The fact that he was brilliant at mathematics did not endear him to his teachers: he arrived at his results not by following the rules they had so painstakingly tried to instil in him, but by what seemed to them like mere guesswork. He boasted he could do six sums in his head to his teacher's one, and the irritating thing was that he was right.

It was a bold man who ever tried to discipline a boy of his size and strength, so he played truant with impunity. He would slip off to the mines – not only the one where his father worked – to hang around with the men who worked the pumping engines and to learn all about them in the process. Soon he had learnt so much he was coming up with ideas to improve them – and found himself much in demand. Before he was nineteen he was selling his expertise to so many different companies that one of them wisely decided to make him their resident engineer. No one was more surprised than his father. 'The boy's much too young!' he protested.

Richard Trevithick.

Until the 1770s the mining companies of Cornwall had been unable to tap the deepest seams of tin or copper because of the water that gathered in the workings. The coming of the steam-engine changed all that. It could drive the necessary pumps and help raise the ore up the shafts. And when the highly efficient engines of James Watt replaced the old Newcomen ones, the mine owners had never been so prosperous. But Watt and his partner Boulton guarded their patent jealously and charged a very high royalty. So the hunt was soon on for engines of similar power that owed nothing to Watt. Trevithick was about to come into his own.

Long before he did so he was asked to go to London to give evidence on behalf of a fellow engineer whom Boulton & Watt had accused of infringing their patent. The case became a *cause célèbre*. But it provoked Trevithick into determining to patent engines of his own one day that would see off the Birmingham firm. By 1800, with his high-pressure engines that did not even use the Watt condenser and were so compact they could be delivered on a simple farm cart, he was well on the way to doing so. But that is to jump ahead. It was at the lawsuit in London in 1791, when he was only twenty, that he met Davies Giddy.

Giddy was a Cornishman too. A bachelor of independent means, he had excelled at Oxford University and was known in London as a cultivated man of letters. He was especially well-informed on matters of science, highly regarded in the intellectual circles in which he moved. He had first heard about Trevithick from a friend of his in Cornwall, Andrew Harvey, a prosperous ironmaster at Hayle. But it was not till he met the young man for himself that he saw in him the makings of such a great engineer that from then on he was to become his intellectual guide and mentor, always ready to supply him with the education he had never had.

In 1797 Richard married the daughter of the iron founder that Giddy knew well, Jane Harvey. Since her father's firm had made the castings for so many of Richard's engines, she had long been attracted by the tireless energy and overwhelming personality of this giant of a man. A brown-haired, open-hearted woman, just a year younger than her husband, she always spoke her mind, had a very strong character and, as doubtless pleased Richard, had one particular advantage over most other women: she was tall enough at least to come up to his chin.

Many years later, in middle age, she delighted in recalling a day, soon after her marriage, when a curious event took place in her kitchen. A friend of hers, Lady Dedunstanville, was there, and her husband, the local squire; Richard had asked them round specially. Here too was his friend, Mr Giddy.

It seemed that for some time now Richard had been working on something that Jane's brother-in-law, William West, a smith, had now made for him. It consisted of an iron container about the size of a kettle which Richard filled with water and placed on the fire. Ordering Giddy to act as stoker, he handed him the bellows and told him to keep the coals white hot. He put Lady Dedunstanville to work too, telling her to release a small cock on the contraption when he gave the word. He now attached to it a pair of tiny wheels and waited for the 'kettle' to boil.

The pressure built up, and on being given the order Lady Dedunstanville released the cock and, in the burst of steam that followed, instantly the wheels started spinning around. Richard was triumphant, maintaining that all it needed now was to carry its own fire and it would travel. Indeed not long afterwards he made another such toy which this time had wheels to stand on. Instead of placing it on the fire he used a red hot poker to set a fire going in the space beneath the boiler and, as Jane was amused to recall, when it had built up enough steam, guess what happened – the thing went running about the table all on its own!

Until the 1790s no one on earth had ever been carried any distance other than by the force of wind or wave, or by the muscle power of man or beast. So when James Watt was developing his steam-engines, he could only describe their different degrees of energy as units of *horsepower*, a measure used ever since. But that mechanical energy too could be harnessed for transport was to most people beyond their comprehension. They might just have understood what a steam-carriage meant if Trevithick had bothered to explain it to them. But they could not have appreciated its significance even after they had seen it in action. But then nor could its inventor.

It made its appearance late in the afternoon on Christmas Eve, 1801, when, as dusk was falling, it was wheeled out of John Tyack's smithy in Camborne. It was cold and raining heavily, so most people were indoors getting ready for Christmas. Had there been any passers-by, they'd have stared in bewilderment.

About the size of a large kettle, standing 15 in. tall by 6 in. wide, this is the actual model engine, now in the Science Museum, London, that Trevithick demonstrated to his wife and friends in his kitchen.

It was as big as a wagon, with a pair of wheels at the back and a smaller pair in front. Curiously, it had a much larger wheel on one side alone that didn't even touch the ground. This was actually the flywheel without which the machine could only have moved forward in jerks on each stroke of the piston. From the cylindrical belly of the beast – the cast-iron boiler slung between the wheels – a tall black chimney stood up which was already emitting smoke, evidently from a fire at the back into which its huge, swarthy master was now shovelling coal.

Soon the boiler, which obtained its water from a cistern at the front, began to vibrate from the steam pressure building up inside. Tyack's workmen realised that Captain Dick as they called him (all the mining engineers were known as Captains) was intending to give the machine they had helped build its first trial. As curious as he was to see how it performed, they asked if they could come with him.

'Jump up,' he cried, as he closed the safety valve to bring all the pressure to bear on the piston in the cylinder which drove the wheels. As the men clambered up to the wooden deck that lay across the top of the boiler, the monstrous vehicle was already moving forward.

In the gathering darkness, with the smoke erupting from the chimney in rhythmic bursts, from the emission of the exhausted steam after each stroke of the piston, it progressed majestically up the hill. And it was a fairly steep hill too. Rising towards Camborne beacon, it crossed the east–west highway which in those days was the only road in the neighbourhood that people other than farmers on carts ever travelled on wheels. Had the cantering horsedriven coach passed along at the time on its way to Penzance, its passengers would not have believed their eyes on seeing coming up on their left this huge, noisy, smoking machine.

The men on board who had made it knew it was in no way threatening. It was just a typically madcap invention of Captain Dick. One of them said afterwards that after crossing 'a roughish piece of road covered with stones, she didn't go quite so fast, and as it was a flood of rain and we were very squeezed together, I jumped off. But she was going faster than I could walk and went on up the hill about half a mile further, when they turned her and came back again.'

That he had been a passenger on the first ever journey by mechanical propulsion – the precursor of the road, rail and air transport machines that would one day characterise a world he could not even have conceived of – did not, of course, occur to him. But then not even Captain Dick could see much future in it either, even though three days later he told the Dedunstanvilles at Tehidy to watch for him tomorrow come steaming up their drive in it all the way from Camborne. Giddy was told too and invited to spend the night there to be present for the great event.

But it never happened. The machine had set off well enough, steered by Richard's cousin, Andrew Vivian, and with Captain Dick as engine-man. On the deck above stood several men, with a lot more walking behind it. Everyone was in festive mood, doubtless looking forward to the celebration that would surely follow on reaching the Dedunstanvilles' stately home. But they had hardly come round the bend, only 400 yards up the hill from where they started, when the steering wheel got caught in a gully to send the entire vehicle toppling on its side into the ditch.

Amazingly no one was hurt. In fact, most people laughed, including Captain Dick who typically could only recommend that all should repair to the nearest public house to console themselves.

This they did – well, it was Christmas, after all. They tucked into a meal of roast goose and enjoyed what Davies Giddy described later as 'proper drinks'. It seems no one even realised they'd forgotten to put out the fire in the engine. By the time they returned to it the water in the boiler had all boiled dry and its red-hot container had set fire to the carriage work above it. Nothing remained but a smouldering heap of blackened wood and crumpled iron.

It had taken over a year to build; scores of men had worked on it and a vast amount of time and money invested. To have abandoned it merely because something on the road had tripped it up? Then walk away and not even dowse the fire? It tells us a lot about the character of Richard Trevithick.

He had discovered on the Christmas Eve outing that it ran well enough to start with. But soon it was using up the steam power it needed more quickly than the boiler could replenish it. It literally ran out of steam and had to stop till the pressure inside could build up again. By taking it up a hill on which horses drawing loads could never do more than walk, and on a slippery surface in 'a flood of rain' which would also have been cooling down the boiler as it drenched it, it's not surprising its strength was overtaxed. Even the railway builders of the next generation did their best not to send their locomotives uphill unless they had to. So over Christmas Trevithick seems to have tried it out again, this time on the level turnpike road. And it must have performed well there or he would not have so confidently told Giddy and the Dedunstanvilles to see him drive up to their house in it the next day.

Having thought he'd fixed it, he had set off with his passengers up the hill and probably discovered it was playing up again. Quick tempered as he was, this could well have irritated him so much that when the steering wheel got caught in the gully and the whole thing toppled over, he could even have been momentarily glad to be shot of the damned thing. Any other inventor would have certainly made sure the fire was out and later resolved to work on the problems that the trials had uncovered.

Richard had such a fertile mind he was always brimming over with ideas for new inventions. But he seemed quite incapable of telling which were likely to prove important and which not. Not that he cared. It was getting the thing to work that mattered; but if that could not be done without detracting from other projects equally exciting, then forget it. Let's go to the pub. He was to show the same lack of persistence two years later when he demonstrated a road carriage in London.

It was his cousin Andrew Vivian who had persuaded him not to give up. He had even bought a share in the patent for the new machine which looked very different from the Camborne one. It had two enormous wheels, nearly eight ft in diameter, with a single small steering wheel at the front. Here the helmsman would sit, with the engineman standing at the rear to feed the fire. Between them, overhead above the boiler as before, there was a deck for the passengers, with the chimney behind them. But this time the piston to turn the driving wheels worked horizontally, not vertically, lunging to and fro out of the boiler towards the feet of the seated helmsman.

Made in Cornwall, it was shipped to London for the coachwork to be added by a firm in Leather Lane. And it was from there, on four successive nights, that the vehicle set forth on properly conducted trials.

From Leather Lane it was to travel along Holborn, up Tottenham Court Road and then west towards Paddington; from there to Mr Lord's cricket ground in the Marylebone fields, and back along much of the same way to return down Gray's Inn Road. To ensure that nothing would impede its measured progress it would make these journeys at night when there was no other traffic around.

So people in bed in Bloomsbury, for instance, might first have just stirred in their sleep at the curious rhythmic thudding, like the menacing beat of approaching muffled drums, floating towards them from nearby Tottenham Court Road – till they woke with a start to hear it pass their house with such a clanking and hissing and clatter that they must have listened fearfully. Anyone who got up to see what it was would have found that by the time he could open his window to peer up the street, it was already round the corner – but he'd have smelt the smoke in the air.

Admittedly in 1803 this was the city's northern suburbs, some of it almost in the country. But there were plenty of people living here who must have been made aware of it. Yet nothing was reported in the press. And apart from the haziest recollections of elderly people who were asked about it many years later, no account survives except that of Andrew Vivian's son, John, aged nineteen, who on one journey was proudly and happily steering it.

They had set off at four in the morning. On the way to Paddington they passed along the side of the Grand Junction Canal which had John thinking 'how deep it was if we should run into it'. Trevithick was engine-man and called out from the back: 'Is she going all right, John?'

'Yes!' he replied delightedly. 'At this rate I think we had better go on to Cornwall!'

They were travelling at six miles an hour at least, maybe more, and suddenly Captain Dick was running alongside. 'Put the helm down, John!' he cried. Before John knew what was

A drawing of the road carriage (from the patent specifications) that Trevithick tried out on the streets of London.

happening, Richard somehow got his foot onto the steering wheel handle and, as John wrote later, 'suddenly we were tearing down six or seven yards of railing from a garden wall, and a person called out from a window: "What the devil are you doing? What is that thing?"'

Whoever it was whose sleep had been disturbed did not wait for an answer; he seems to have just slammed the window shut and gone back to bed. They got the carriage back to Leather Lane where it was reckoned that 'a great cause of difficulty was the fire-bars working loose, letting the fire fall through into the ash-pan. When steam was up she went capitally well, but not when the fire-bars dropped.'

Whatever had gone wrong – and young John could hardly be relied on to know – engineers today do not believe that any of the problems were insuperable, certainly not that of the fire-bars. The accident to the railings had more to do with young John's steering than anything at fault with the engine. In all important respects the trials had been a big success. Yet once again Trevithick became impatient over an unexpected setback and put his mind to other things. The fact that they had also run out of money would not have deterred a more tenacious inventor either.

A new idea, however, occurred to him. Since the huge wheels with their flatter circumference had gripped the smoother streets of London much more effectively than the smaller ones had the unmade-up surfaces of the Cornish roads, it might run even better on rails. But rails could only set it on a pre-determined course, and what use is a vehicle that cannot even choose the way it wants to go? In industry perhaps? To carry products to the nearest port or canal? This was generally done on railways anyway, in wagons drawn by horses. The ironmasters of South Wales, who had bought many of his stationary engines, used just such tramways for this purpose. So he mentioned his idea to one of them he knew.

Samuel Homfray had such faith in Trevithick after installing one of his engines to drive his blast-furnaces that he had acquired a stake in them himself. They were not only being used by his competitors in foundries, but in collieries and mills in many parts of the country. He reckoned that whatever the cost of investment, if it would give him a share in the profits from Richard's patents, it was a gamble worth taking.

And he loved gambling. Though rich enough from his profits as an ironmaster to lose considerable amounts of money without being seriously incommoded, he seems to have had an intuitive understanding of what was a good bet, and

Trevithick engines were definitely that. So when Richard suggested that the wagons drawn by horses, which all the foundries in the district used to transport their iron to the Glamorgan canal at Abercynon, could be better hauled by a steam-engine, he was immediately interested. Soon he was so excited by what he learnt that he rashly told a fellow ironmaster, Anthony Hill, he'd bet five hundred guineas on a Trevithick engine hauling ten tons of iron from Penydaren to Abercynon without even pausing for breath. It was a vast amount of money to put at risk, but whenever Homfray gambled it was always for the highest possible stakes.

So if only to win Mr Homfray's bet for him, Richard began again to turn another idea of his into a practical reality. The castings for his locomotive were made by his wife's family's foundry, engineered by her brother-in-law and delivered by wagon to South Wales. For five days, to the fascination of the neighbourhood, he conducted trials till at last he was satisfied it could meet the challenge set for it.

On that day a big crowd turned up to watch. Before them on the tramway stood this strange iron horse which seemed already to be champing at the bit, snorting and trembling from the pressure building up in its belly. Into the hungry mouth of the fire beneath it, the giant from Cornwall who had given birth to this monster was shovelling coal, while from its tall black chimney it breathed clouds of smoke into the air. Sometimes perhaps an explosive burst of steam had the onlookers step back in alarm. If the men who normally led the horses along the track to draw the wagons to Abercynon were here, they'd have been far too fascinated just then to worry that this machine could put them all out of work.

Presently Mr Homfray arrived with the ironmaster, Anthony Hill, who had taken on his bet. The wagons, each laden with a quantity of iron, had already been attached to the engine, the first including room for the two passengers.

Homfray was eager for the start. He had placed enough bets in his time, but never one quite as exciting as this. Doubtless he cheerfully reminded Captain Dick he had five hundred guineas at stake, while his companion was probably looking back at the wagons, trying to judge whether they were really carrying ten tons of iron. Homfray was so confident he would have willingly had a few more hitched on.

Then Richard pulled a lever to send rings of smoke juddering noisily up from the chimney. A hiss of steam, and slowly the big wheels began to turn. As the procession of wagons began to gather speed and onlookers realised it would soon be out of sight, was it then that one of them went dashing towards the retreating train to clamber aboard, followed instantly by others doing the same? In a letter to Giddy afterwards Richard said seventy extra men got aboard which vastly increased the weight it was carrying. Soon they were travelling at least as fast as a trotting horse and, with the engine showing no sign of strain, Captain Dick opened it up. For the passengers, nothing they'd experienced could have been as exhilarating as this, in spite of the smoke that got into their eyes and the shaking of the wagons as they sped along.

But suddenly they were nearly thrown off. Richard had brought the train to an abrupt halt. Just yards away there were large boulders lying on the line.

Possibly there had been a storm the night before which had caused a landslip. Certainly there were obstacles in their way that no one had anticipated. But fortunately, there were enough men on board to clear the 'large rocks', as Trevithick described them; he said there was even a tree to be removed. But it meant that instead of completing the journey in less than two hours, which even at only five miles an hour they should easily have done, it took more than twice as long. Nevertheless, it comfortably delivered its load to the Glamorgan canal and Anthony Hill conceded that he owed Mr Homfray five hundred guineas.

A working replica of Trevithick's Penydaren locomotive, subsequently modified for the one built at Gateshead, made for the Welsh Industrial & Maritime Museum.

Richard had hoped Davies Giddy would be there for the occasion. He had urgently begged him to come. He knew his business rivals would look for any excuse to sneer at his achievement, and this would be avoided if the highly respected Mr Giddy could witness the event and publicise it in the influential circles in which he moved. But Giddy had recently been persuaded to stand for Parliament and was busy with those who wanted to put him up for the constituency of Helston in Cornwall. So he had been unable to get there. And perhaps that was just as well. For halfway home on the triumphal return journey, the track now free of all obstacles to give them a fast, clear run, a bolt broke off beneath the boiler and all the water gushed out.

So there the thing stood, blocking the tramway, an immovable heap of iron. And when it was discovered that the rails it had travelled on had buckled under its weight in several places, the men who led the horse-drawn wagons knew that, much as they had enjoyed the trip, their jobs were safe after all.

This time Richard did persist, at least for a while. He sent imploring letters to Giddy urging him to trumpet the success he had had. And after making the necessary repairs, he hung about for weeks for two government engineers he expected. They were men that Homfray had persuaded to check out the machine for themselves and subject it to whatever tests they wanted. But they never showed up. Meanwhile, Jane had been writing to Richard regularly from Cornwall wanting to know when he was ever coming home.

Once the damage to the tramway had been repaired, he managed to make further journeys. On one occasion he hauled twenty-five tons with ease. But the rails gave way so often that in the end he gave up. He took the wheels off the engine and let Homfray have it to drive a hammer in his foundry. He knew from the start it could have such a use. Typical of the innate lack of belief in himself that he showed so often, he had even designed it that way in case it failed as a locomotive.

That autumn another of his locomotives, built to almost the same design, was demonstrated at Gateshead on the Tyne. It had been engineered by John Steel, a one-time millwright in Cornwall whom Jane Trevithick remembered as having a wooden leg. Her husband best knew him for the work he had done in helping him build the engine for Samuel Homfray.

Steel was now working in Newcastle and, after the success of his friend's locomotive at Penydaren, was sure it had a future in the north. He at least believed in it. So Richard re-designed it, and after it had been built in Gateshead he went up there to see it demonstrated.

As at Penydaren, it aroused huge local interest. It had been asked for by a colliery looking for an alternative to horse-drawn wagons to get its coal from the pithead to the Tyne. Other collieries were represented too at the trials. But while it was put through its paces on a specially constructed track, they could see for themselves that their own tramways would never take its weight. And what was so wrong with horses anyway?

However, among those watching was a young man that Trevithick may well have got to meet that day; certainly they met somewhere somehow at that time. Little did the father of the locomotive guess, though, that this young Geordie, whose accent must have made him as difficult to understand as his own Cornish brogue made him, would one day – not so far off either – be covered in the glory that could equally, perhaps more deservedly, have been his.

Still, it has to be stated in all fairness that on that day the Geordie, George Stephenson, didn't know it either.

CHAPTER THREE

The Rock Attacked

The port of Arbroath did not naturally breed seamen. Even fishing was carried on somewhere else, up the coast at Auchmithie where there wasn't even a quay. Admittedly, there'd always been a harbour, replaced by a bigger one in the 1740s, but the men of Arbroath who sailed from it were vastly outnumbered by those who stayed at home to work on dry land.

Weaving was the local industry. Walk beside the Brothock, the fast narrow river that runs through the town, and from most nearby cottages in 1800 you'd hear the constant thud of looms; and on the public greens see the yarn to be woven, saturated in the pure clear water of the Brothock, hanging up over lines and poles to be exposed for weeks and weeks to the bleaching effects of wind and weather.

Their raw material was flax; and it was this that the ships set forth every spring to fetch from the Baltic countries where it grew in abundance. In winter, when the Baltic ports were mostly iced up, the mariners turned to weaving themselves.

Everyone was at it. The invention of spinning machines had meant yarn could be produced far more quickly than it could be woven into cloth; and since no one yet had found a way to mechanise looms, the home weavers were still very much in demand. From the flax and hemp the ships brought in, the weavers made linen, canvas and sailcloth that the merchants exported not only back to Scandinavia, but to Glasgow, London and America and, till the war with France put a stop to it, to western Europe too.

So despite the recession that the war had brought about, the merchants of Arbroath were doing well. From the Baltic alone they imported over 1,000 tons of flax and hemp every year, and they sold so successfully what they exported in return that one firm had an Arbroathian living permanently in Latvia as their agent, while in 1801 another, though only eighteen at the time, was running a highly profitable export-import agency in Gothenberg.

There were plenty, therefore, who could afford the smart houses on the fashionable stretch of the High Street, the only part that was paved, between the

Parish Kirk and the shore, especially if they were content to have them built of sandstone. Since the abandonment of the Abbey in the 1590s, builders had regarded its red sandstone walls as a free local quarry. It was plunder that reduced it to the ruin it is today. By 1800 most of it had been recycled into the walls of the town's houses and cottages.

Till recently, in what had once been the house of the medieval Abbot, a textile factory had not only supplied the home-weavers with their yarn but on their own looms produced linen and hosiery themselves. New mills were starting up, powered by water-wheels driven by the Brothock. They obtained their labour from the scores of single men flocking in from the depressed countryside around. These vagrant labourers had their own doss-houses and looked for work wherever they could get it. By 1806, when Robert arrived here to set up his base, the population of the town had risen from a mere 2,000 in 1750 to four times as many now.

Arbroath in 1823. The smoking chimneys of the town's now industrialised textile industry illustrate the changes since Robert began building the lighthouse.

To mark their growing importance, a splendid new Town House had recently been built on the High Street comprising Town Hall, Council offices and Court. Here the Provost and Town Clerk expressed their approval of Robert's plan to put a light on the dangerous Bell Rock and offered him free use of the harbour.

But they were probably more interested just then in the visit of another engineer, the famous James Watt, now seventy, who came up from his works in Birmingham specially to supervise the installation of one of his steam-engines in a mill that had hitherto been powered by a water-wheel. That within ten years the town would be dominated by the smoking chimneys of its mechanised mills might possibly have been guessed by Robert, but not that steam power could be of any use to him in building a lighthouse.

He made a list of his priorities. The first was to organise what he referred to as the Floating Light. The Parliamentary Bill had stipulated that, as soon as work on the rock began, some kind of light should be set up, on a floating buoy perhaps, so that light dues could be charged to passing ships long before the lighthouse itself was completed, the income to be used at once to start paying back the loan.

Robert had grander ideas for it. He wanted a large, fully manned lightship permanently moored near the rock which could also be used for the men's living quarters. That labourers would not be going to work from their homes, but in rowing boats from a wave-tossed ship eleven miles out to sea, was not yet appreciated in Arbroath.

For conversion into his lightship, Robert acquired a Prussian fishing boat that had been captured in the war against Napoleon. He had it rebuilt to his own design and named it the *Pharos*. But to make sure it would not be blown onto the rock by one of the frequent gales that got up, it would have to be moored more than a mile away from it. This would mean a very long row for his men every day.

And suppose in such a gale they found themselves on the rock and it was impossible for the boats to be rowed any distance at all? And suppose the tide should overflow them? There had to be a refuge to which all could cling in such a dire emergency. He had in mind a wooden hut to stand on stilts above the highest tides. It could act as a beacon to shipping, and might even in time be enlarged to become the men's regular home. That they might be imprisoned while a storm raged around them in a wooden shack perched in the air above a perilous sea, was also not something as yet anticipated by the potential labour force in Arbroath.

Rennie was suspicious. Though graciously conceding that 'should this project fail, the expense of the experiment cannot be great,' he kept dwelling on the

Eddystone, saying 'it is better to follow what was found to be an answer there than in a work so important look for other methods that have not stood the test of time'. Having received Robert's working drawings which showed his own particular way to dovetail the stones, Rennie replied that 'when we meet, I trust you will either convince me of the superiority of your plan or I shall satisfy you respecting Mr Smeaton's'. But he did not satisfy Robert who had clearly decided that, though he would always listen to his chief's advice, he would not necessarily act on it. And he rarely did. After a decision had been made to use Aberdeen granite for the tower, Rennie informed him: 'I have heard from one whose opinion is not to be highlighted that there is not one building of any considerable age in Aberdeen that does not exhibit symptoms of decay.' Robert checked it out and simply replied that Aberdeen granite 'seems to be everlasting in its nature'.

After putting in hand the Floating Light, Robert's next priority was to find somewhere in Arbroath, close to the harbour, for a workyard. On what is today the site of the town's school on Ladyloan, he was offered land on lease at twenty guineas a year. Though Robert thought the rent excessive, he signed the contract and on the same day contracted with an Aberdeen quarry for his granite.

Though it would be a long time yet before the stones would arrive, he was already considering how to transport them from the quay to the yard, as each would weigh almost a ton. Remembering, perhaps from his military exercises in Edinburgh, a gun-carriage used by the artillery, a kind of bottomless cart with tackle to raise and carry cannon just high enough to clear the ground, he reckoned this sling-cart, as it was called, could easily be adapted to carrying his stones one by one to the yard and back again to the quay when cut to shape.

To ship them to the rock, he ordered from a boatyard at Leith a vessel he designed to meet all their needs. Rennie was doubtless delighted to hear he had named it the *Smeaton*. But as it would not be able to tie up on the rock itself, other craft would have to get the ton-weight stones ashore. He thought of the flat-bottomed wide-beamed dinghy that the Norwegians who invented it call a praam.

Despite a flourishing boat-building yard in Arbroath, he seems to have had his praams made in Leith where certainly his sling-cart was made – and where he also engaged a man called James Craw, and his horse Bassey, to draw it. Even work of this nature he did not offer in the town where it would have to be done.

Unlike his wife and the rest of the women at Baxters Place, Robert never let sentiment influence his judgement. He was not unfeeling, far from it, as events will show, but always it was the quality of the work he might expect that mattered most. That particularly applied to masons. To ensure that in stormy weather

The sling cart, with James Craw and his horse Bassey who hauled each one of the 2,835 stones from the workyard to the harbour.

Unloading stones from a praam on to a landing stage at the rock.

waves would dispel their fury into the air rather than against the structure itself, he had designed his lighthouse with sloping sides, tapering up towards the top in a sweeping parabolic curve. This meant that each of its ninety courses would be smaller than the one beneath it, requiring different shaped stones at each level. To achieve the necessary accuracy, Robert hired a craftsman he knew, James Slight, to make wooden moulds from his patterns into each of which the appropriate stone when cut must fit exactly, or it would have to be junked and replaced by a new one.

No wonder he wanted the best possible stone-cutters. He'd have known there were masons to be had in Arbroath, but it was the men who had built for him before that he wanted, even if most of them lived in Aberdeen. He would pay them good money and in his workyard provide living quarters for them and their keep.

Not that such men were to be signed on yet. First he needed an efficient Clerk of Works to take charge of the yard. A young man called David Logan, highly

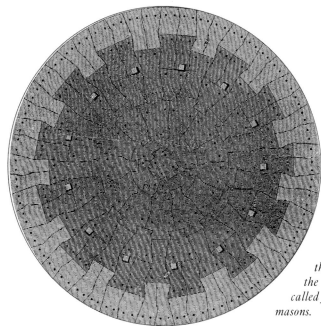

This jigsaw of dovetailed interlocking stones, of sandstone surrounded by an outer ring of granite, was the design for just one of the lower foundation courses. To cut the stones to the many different shapes that the templates (below) required called for great skill from the masons.

recommended by James Haldane, so impressed Robert he even agreed to interview his father, Peter Logan, as possible Foreman on the rock. Peter was invited to breakfast at Baxters Place and not only got the job, but persuaded Robert to take on a friend of his from Aberdeen, Francis Watt, to be in charge of all joinery work.

In this way the team was formed – either personally recommended, or men he had worked with before and knew he could trust, such as Captain Sinclair whom he made Master of the *Pharos*, or John Reid whom he appointed as its lightkeeper, or Captain Wilson to whom he gave the vitally important job of Landing Master, in charge of all the rowing boat movements between the parent ship and the rock. No man was recruited locally, not even his blacksmith.

Blacksmith? A meticulous forward planner, Robert had anticipated that in hacking out the rock for the lighthouse foundations pickaxes would become rapidly blunted. To keep them sharp, a smith would be needed. Having heard about this, a young man in Brechin called James Dove offered his services. Since leaving school he'd been carrying on his trade wherever he could and was thinking of setting up in business in Montrose, but could not help feeling that he might do just as well 'by serving a good master'. More than once he had tried to see Robert in Arbroath, but always missed him. Impressed by his determination, and knowing most smiths would be horrified at the idea of setting up a forge in a place that would be under water within an hour or so of starting work, Robert took him on. Always a shrewd judge of character, he could see that Dove was just the man to respond to a challenge.

In March 1807 Robert was saying he hoped to start work on the rock by mid-May at latest, but that would depend on the Floating Light, the *Pharos*, being in position by then and the *Smeaton* ready to act as their supply vessel. At that time there was not much sign of either being ready, so he was getting anxious.

By then word had got about in Arbroath that men taken on would be housed on a ship. Few had ever been to sea before, and whatever unease they felt was in no way helped by learning they would not be allowed to come home for at least a month. Doubtless in the public houses they wondered why not; and possibly an ex-seaman among them, James Glen, now a joiner, gave an answer. To judge by what we know of this man later, he delighted in telling lurid tales about the terrors of life at sea and might well have warned them how seasick they were all going to be.

It was indeed for this reason that Robert had insisted they must all stay a month. He knew that even in summer a boat anchored off the rock would pitch and roll every night, but he reckoned after a month they would have found their sea-legs and be happy to go on working there.

What he did not anticipate was that another of his requirements was to prove a far bigger obstacle to recruitment. He expected them to work on Sundays.

His wife and mother would have been shocked that he considered for a moment that they should. If God Himself had taken a rest after six days building the entire universe, Robert could surely not expect his men to imperil their immortal souls for the sake of a mere lighthouse.

Naturally he never told the family. He understood their thinking but reckoned that if God was the architect of the universe He would surely consider it absurd, if not positively sinful, to ignore the chance to get on with this life-saving work when the rock was only even visible for two out of every twelve hours. So to reassure the men that they would not be risking their chance of salvation, he asked a Minister he knew in Edinburgh to compose a special prayer that could be said – while also making it known that for work on Sundays wages would be doubled.

On 9 July the *Pharos* was ready at last. It had berths for thirty workmen and crew; quarters for the Master, Mate, Lightkeeper and Foreman; a cabin for Robert; and a galley. But not being designed for sailing – it was, after all, just the Floating Light that Robert always called it – it had to be brought direct to its position off the rock where, after many attempts, it was at last successfully anchored.

Knowing how much it would pitch and roll, Robert planned to keep his men on the *Smeaton* first till they had become, as he put it, 'sea-hardy'. The fact that on this vessel they would have nowhere to sleep but in hammocks slung in the hold, and nowhere to eat but in a makeshift caboose on deck, would make them eager for the relative comforts that awaited them on the lightship. And since the *Smeaton* could anchor close inshore, the Landing Master, Wilson, could teach the men how to handle the rowing-boats over a very short distance before they had to undertake the mile-long row that would be required on each trip from the *Pharos*.

At present the *Smeaton* was still in Leith, and Robert had become angrily impatient. When at last it did arrive, he went out on it at once with half a dozen men and his foreman Peter Logan to find landing places on the rock for rowing-boats and a ledge for the forge, and to make all the preparations they could. Back in Arbroath the vast amount of stores and equipment ordered was delivered to the quay, the inventory including such items as japanned quart tankards, frying pans, tinder boxes, 'two tables each 17 ft long, 8 gals linseed oil', and 'coals for the smith'.

Still not having heard if the men he had picked would work on Sundays, Robert took their silence for acquiescence. But he decided not to risk a Sunday sailing as planned. He would go the next day on the late evening tide in the hope of arriving for the first low tide on the rock next morning when work could at last begin.

At the Parish Kirk on the Sunday the Minister said special prayers to bless the expedition and by the following evening the *Smeaton* was ready to sail, proudly flying her colours. The other ships in the harbour flew theirs, and as the twenty-four workmen who'd been hired went aboard, it seemed the whole town had come down to see them off. Among them was surely James Spink, the popular captain of the mail boat, distinctive in his characteristic jacket and blue flat bonnet. The men knew he'd be bringing them their letters every week and, as Robert had promised to pay for the postage, their families expected letters back.

The *Smeaton* cast off and as it cleared the harbour, such cheers went up from the deck and on the quay that, as Robert reported later, 'in the still of the evening they must have been heard in all parts of the town, re-echoing from the walls and lofty turrets of the venerable Abbey itself'.

He went on deck. From their quarters below came the sound of the men singing, most of them happily drunk on what they had put away in the taverns before they left. Later, in his cabin, he could hear the helmsman on deck singing wistfully a song he recognised: 'There's a Providence sits up aloft to keep watch for poor Jack.'

Deep from his heart he prayed to that Providence himself.

Exactly one week earlier, from an address in Limehouse on the Thames in London, Richard Trevithick had written to his friend Davies Giddy to tell him he'd just signed a contract with the Thames Archway Company and was so grateful to Giddy 'for putting him in the way of it'.

The company had engaged him to bore a tunnel under the Thames from Rotherhithe across to Limehouse in order to serve the new docks such as Rennie and others had now built for the busy and expanding port of London. Work had actually begun two years earlier when another engineer from Cornwall, Robert Vazie, was given the job. He had managed to dig a shaft over 75 ft deep – a remarkable feat, with no machinery – but had to give up when it filled with water and quicksands. The company blamed him and, when Giddy heard they were looking for a replacement, he quickly recommended Trevithick, eager to make amends for not having been able to publicise his success at Penydaren.

At first the two Cornishmen worked together, but they soon parted company and Trevithick was put in sole charge. It was a happy time for him. It did not bother him at all that not even on Tyneside had anyone except the young enginewright he'd met there been interested in his locomotive. Trevithick recalled later they got on so well that he dandled the young man's son on his knee. Even more uneducated, in fact almost illiterate, George Stephenson had just lost his wife and was trying to bring up their three-year-old boy on his own. Not expecting to hear of him ever again, Richard wished him luck with his engineering ambitions and came south to London.

His wife and family – he was the father of four children by now – had seen little of him in the preceding eighteen months. When he was marooned in Wales trying to retrieve the fortunes of his Penydaren locomotive, Jane had crossly asked when he was ever coming home. He had replied by suggesting she should bring the family to him in Wales. That certainly shut her up; she had never left Cornwall and never intended to.

While John Steel was rebuilding his locomotive at Gateshead, Richard was home for a while but very restless, and off to Tyneside whenever he was needed. Now, after finally getting shot of locomotive engines altogether, leaving the field wide open to the likes of young George Stephenson, he wrote to his wife from London to tell her excitedly of his contract with the Thames tunnel company.

Everything, he thought, was now going so well for him. His stationary engines were earning him good royalties (though he was so unbusinesslike most of them went uncollected). And he had recently been contracted by Trinity House to adapt an engine of his to power a dredger on the Thames. For this he would be paid sixpence for every ton of silt he could remove. He accepted with alacrity; it would be a nice little earner, asking very little back from him in return. And now, as he told Davies Giddy in his letter of August 1807, he had got the tunnelling contract as well.

It's not as if he were being asked to engineer as yet any more than a narrow tube, a mere driftway, a bore less than 3 ft wide and 5 ft high. When completed it would later be expanded into the full-sized tunnel required. He was sure it could not possibly take more than nine months at most. Once he had hired the necessary miners to do the excavating from the bottom of Robert Vazie's shaft, he did not expect to have to spend more than an hour or two at most each day on the site.

But he was missing his wife and family. On his rare visits home he often talked of how rich they were all going to be from the use of his many patents, while his wife just wondered how they were going to find the money for their next meal. But he needed her and, once installed in lodgings in Rotherhithe, he begged her to bring the family up to stay with him there. His ship was about to come home at last.

What he probably did not reveal to her was that under his contract he was to receive £1,000 on completing the tunnel, half to be paid on getting halfway across. If at any time the company decided to pull out, he would get £500. But if he pulled out himself – or found the job to be impossible – he would get nothing at all.

CHAPTER FOUR

Beneath the Thames

It's 23 August 1807, six days after the *Smeaton* set sail from Arbroath. Everyone is now on board the *Pharos* as originally intended. It's 8 a.m., their first Sunday at sea.

'Almighty and ever blessed God, thou art not confined to temples made with hands. The temple most acceptable to thee is the heart of thy worshipper. Even here where no temple invites, be with us and strengthen us to discharge the duties of thy holy day.'

Robert is intoning the prayer the Edinburgh minister composed for him. Before him stand his men, heads bare, solemn and respectful; with them, Captain Sinclair and his crew, lightkeeper John Reid, landing master Wilson and foreman Peter Logan. An awning has been raised to give the semblance of a chapel. At the top of the companionway the ship's Bible has been reverently placed.

The bell had rung half an hour earlier to wake the ship's company to attend Divine Service before breakfast. Low tide on that day was not till mid-morning, by which time Robert hoped every man would be working on the rock. And that would depend on the effect of the minister's prayer.

So far all had gone well. The sea had been no more than restless and few had been seasick – thanks perhaps to what Nature itself had provided to prevent it. On his very first landing on the rock with Haldane, Robert had noticed the dulse, a red, edible seaweed that was known to be an antidote to sea-sickness. On their first visit to the rock everyone had picked it in quantity.

Work that morning had meant hacking out the place for James Dove's forge, clearing seaweed and cutting drains from the pools left by the tide. But on their next visit they were told by Robert to start boring holes for a pyramid of six huge oak timbers, to be floated out to them from Arbroath, which once erected would serve as a beacon to mark the rock for ships at sea and support a cabin above the highest tide as a refuge for all if ever needed. No wonder the men worked hard at it.

'The Sabbath was appointed to celebrate thy creating power, whose word spake the universe into being. Let not the circumstances in which we are now placed be permitted to wean our affections from thy worship, while being called to labour in the service of humanity even on this day of rest.'

Encouraged by a loud 'Amen', Robert reckoned he would not be short-handed. But after breakfast, four men came to tell him that despite the prayer and much searching of their consciences, they still felt the Sabbath to be sacrosanct.

The relatively calm weather they enjoyed made no difference to the undulating swell that marked the waters where the *Pharos* was stationed. Just to get from the deck into the rowing boats, swinging and bobbing alongside, was no mean feat for men not accustomed to the sea. Landing master Wilson had his work cut out in cajoling and bullying them. It didn't help that James Dove was so possessive about his enormous bellows. Its awkward shape, and the coal he needed too, made up a cumbersome cargo that the men much resented having to carry on every trip.

Although the distance to be rowed was four times longer than that from the *Smeaton*, they had got into the swing of it and were more bored than tired. To relieve the tedium, Robert suggested their two boats might have races with each other. This was eagerly taken up. The badinage between the crews that resulted and the shanties they sang while rowing expressed the high morale of them all.

As Robert anticipated, on the *Smeaton* they had found their sea-legs so they could handle the constant rolling of the *Pharos*. And they were as pleased with the mattressed bunks to sleep on as they were with the fully equipped galley and expert ship's cook, an Italian, who fed them. On their nightly rum ration they would, said Robert, 'sing, dance and smoke as if they were at home'. Alone in his cabin he would sometimes hear them telling wildly improbable stories to each other. Always there was music. One, he realised, had brought a flute with him; another, a violin.

On the rock, those not drilling the holes for the beacon house timbers were levelling the ground where the lighthouse would stand, soon to start hacking out the 44 ft wide circle that would take the foundations. Dove was kept so busy sharpening picks he was often still at it as the tide flowed in around his feet. Sometimes it was up to his knees before he responded to the urgent calls from the others and made for the boats with his enormous bellows, as the sea engulfed his fire in a hiss of steam.

One day the *Smeaton*, now working as the supply ship it was meant to be, came out with eight extra men Robert needed. It was a windy day and the rowing-boat that landed them had only just got back to the ship when a sudden squall got up and drove it from its moorings with the rowing-boat attached to it. No way could it get back in time to fetch its men before the tide had overflowed the rock.

So Robert found himself marooned with thirty-four men and only boats enough for twenty-six. 'The solemnity of the group when they saw the perilous predicament we were in,' he was later to write, 'made an impression never to be effaced. They just looked steadfastly on me in the most perfect silence. Not a word was uttered.'

Already the tide was flowing in around them and Robert found that, whatever ideas he may have had, 'my mouth was so parched my tongue refused utterance.' So he lapped some water from one of the pools, and as he did so he heard a voice cry out – 'A boat! A boat!' It was the mail packet, with Mr Spink himself at the helm, passing close to the rock on its way to bring them their letters. Even then it was a race against time to get everyone away before the rock was submerged.

Once back on the *Pharos*, eight men decided, not surprisingly, that they would not go to work on the rock next morning. And as Robert bitterly reflected, very soon now, after a month on the job, they would all be entitled to go home for good. As if to make sure they did, it was just then that the restless sea finally decided to unleash its power.

By midnight a gale was blowing of such force that, as Robert recorded:

. . . every wave which struck caused all on board to tremble. Twice I was thrown upon the floor. About two o'clock a heavy sea came pouring down into the berths, and the motion of the ship being suddenly deadened by the flowing in of water, I doubt there was anyone who did not think the vessel was in the act of sinking. I groped my way to the galley where several men were loudly employed in prayer, while others protested that if they somehow survived no one would ever see them afloat again. The Captain assured me we would soon have better weather, but every approaching wave looked as if it would overwhelm us. On deck I found one solitary individual – the seaman on watch who was wearing no greatcoat or overall of any kind. He had lashed himself to the mast and told me with a smile that he intended to wet as few clothes as possible so he'd have a dry shift when he went below. Seeing the confidence of these gentlemen, and the smile of the watchman though lashed to the foremast, I suddenly felt myself perfectly at ease.

Two days later the gale had blown itself out, enabling the *Smeaton* to bring them much needed supplies. If the men protested at what they had been made to endure, it seems as if they also felt that if they could come through that, they could come through anything. So when their month was up, all but one agreed to

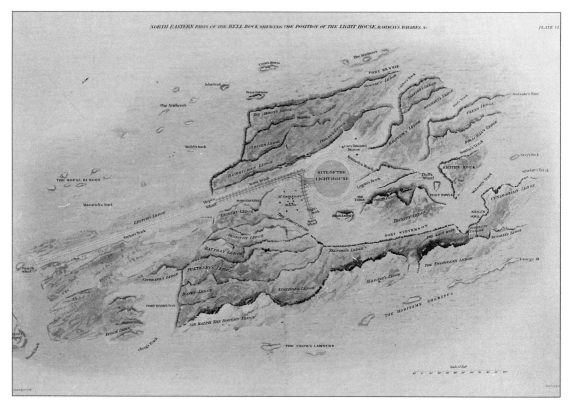

A map of the site drawn by Robert, marking the lighthouse, railway, beacon house and landing stages, and naming the many different inlets, rocks and coves after men connected with the work.

stay. And the four who had so stalwartly defended the sanctity of the Sabbath let Robert know that they would now agree to work on God's day but on one condition – that they should not be paid for it.

The *Smeaton* now delivered the six 50 ft long timbers that were to form the pyramid for the beacon house. They were towed in at high tide and left to subside with the lowering water till they rested on the surface of the rock. By then the men were already there to receive them, standing up to their waists in the water, their number now increased by twenty-six others who had come out to help – the team of carpenters and joiners led by Francis Watt.

Under Watt's direction, before the tide had even finally ebbed, they were raising with the aid of a derrick two of the great beams to lean against each other at the top while the base of each was inserted deep into the hole prepared for it. While some drove in the necessary wedges to hold them firm, others erected two more of the stanchions the same way to form a four-sided cone. It was a frantic race against time. But whatever the hurry, Robert had to ensure that each timber was absolutely secure in its pre-excavated base. When the cone was at last erected, with its four sloping uprights meeting at the top some 30 ft above the highest tide, a huge cheer went up. Almost up to their necks now in water as they waded back to their boats, they knew there was now something solid in place to cling to if caught by the tide.

Next day they got the other two stanchions up to turn the cone into a six-sided pyramid, its legs driven deep and tight into the rock. While the original team went back to hacking out the lighthouse foundations, Watt's joiners began making a platform in the pyramid a few ft above the highest tide. As soon as completed, James Dove took possession of part of it as a permanent base for his forge, so there'd be no more carrying of his coal and bellows to and fro in the boats. And on the rest of the deck there was room for the joiners to go on building the beacon house whatever the sea did beneath them.

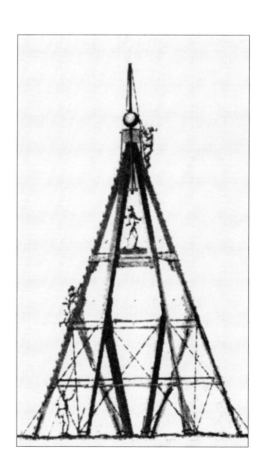

Something to cling to – the pyramid of timbers that became the framework for the beacon house.

On 3 October a flag was hoisted to tell ships at sea that it marked the position of the dreaded Bell Rock which at night could also be distinguished by the light beaming out from the *Pharos*. Two days later another ship anchored in these waters, signalling to Robert that the Chief Engineer had arrived to inspect progress.

Robert found Rennie on board with his teenage son, George. They were on their way up north – for Rennie to check on the progress of his harbour works at Fraserburgh – and thought they would drop by, as it were. Next morning Robert took them to the rock where Rennie was clearly a bit nervous about the lapping water all around him, as he admitted later in his Report to the Commissioners:

> We remained on the rock for about one and a half hours when the tide began to flow rather quickly so we returned to our vessel . . . Considerable progress has been made and I hope by next June the rock will be ready to receive the foundation course of the lighthouse. I do not want to state particularly when this most essential object will be completed but I have great confidence in the zeal Mr Stevenson has shown and know he will do all he can to expedite the work.

With winter coming on, when the weather would make it impossible to work on the rock at all, work now ceased for the next four months. Robert took Rennie to inspect the yard in Arbroath where the workshops and other buildings were now completed and Peter Logan's son, David, as Clerk of Works, was already receiving the first stones from the quarries. On hearing that Scotland's most famous engineer was in their midst, the Provost and Town Council of Arbroath made a huge fuss of him and honoured his visit by presenting him with the Freedom of the Burgh.

On 4 December Robert went back to his family whom he had not seen for over three months. In July, another boy had been born they named Alan. His brother Thomas and twin sister Elizabeth were each four; of the other two girls, the eldest was a healthy six-year old, her slightly younger sister, Janet, not quite so robust. On Christmas Day Robert wrote to Peter Logan, apologising that he was obliged 'to go a few miles into the country today,' presumably with his family. But he was back at work next morning, writing more business letters in one of which he mentioned lightly that his children were 'all now at work with the whooping cough, having just got over the measles!' By adding in the very next line that his wife sent her compliments, he suggested that neither was in any way particularly anxious.

*

In 1807 Jane Trevithick's children were much the same age. Although her husband had been begging her to bring them to London, and though she had seen even less of him over the last two years than Jeannie in Edinburgh had seen of Robert, the thought of uprooting herself from Cornwall to live in London of all places was even more daunting than that of joining him in Wales as he'd once asked her to.

Backed by her brother, who strongly advised against it, she wrote regularly to Richard to say it was out of the question. But he needed her, he said. So in the end, with her four children, the youngest just a baby, she travelled 300 miles in the post-chaise, with all the overnight stops at coaching inns the journey entailed, to arrive exhausted at her husband's lodgings in Rotherhithe. As one of her sons recalled many years later, 'the contrast between her clean, fresh Cornish home and the dingy habitation at Rotherhithe did not help remove the fatigue of the journey.'

Cramped space for a miner in Trevithick's tunnel.

Soon she discovered in her husband's pocket two unopened letters of hers. Hurt and angry, she demanded an explanation. 'I knew they'd only give more reasons for not coming,' he told her bitterly, 'so I had not the heart to read them.'

In London she had no friends. Even Davies Giddy was not often there, member of Parliament though he was. A bachelor whom everyone thought would remain so, he had recently fallen for a lady in Eastbourne whom he was now steadfastly courting. Down there at least as much as ever in Cornwall among the constituents who had elected him their MP, he was only in London when the House required his presence.

Depressed as she was in Rotherhithe, among Londoners who probably found her Cornish accent as incomprehensible as she found theirs, Jane was later to make friends with a Frenchwoman even more lonely and unhappy. A refugee that the French Revolution had driven from the luxury she had once enjoyed, she had married a Cornishman and through him got to meet Jane Trevithick. The two women consoled each other, with homemade Cornish pasties at one home, and French cuisine at the other.

Richard kept telling his wife how rich they were all going to be very soon. His dredger on the Thames was earning good money; his patented engines entitled him to royalties that often his customers actually paid him; and any day now he'd get £1,000 from the completion of the first ever tunnel to be driven under a major river.

He had every reason to be optimistic. Tunnelling had begun on the same day that Robert Stevenson and his team had set sail for Bell Rock. Progress had been good. They had been advancing over six ft a day; by mid-October, almost twelve; and this despite the fact there was only room at the face for one miner at a time, stooping as he had to with his pick or shovel, while behind him someone else had to squeeze a heavy barrow past the men boarding up the sides and roof, and all working in foul air and by flickering candlelight.

By 21 December they had gone 947 ft, almost three-quarters of the way. Admittedly they were now meeting what Richard described as man-made rock, meaning compressed sedimentary deposits that geologists today would call calcareous stone, and he was worried about what might lie behind it once they had broken through. But by January they were beyond the low water mark the other side and bringing the bore uphill towards the surface. There seemed little doubt they would complete the job long before the nine months were up.

On the afternoon of 26 January Jane Trevithick was horrified to see her husband come home without shoes or hat, his shirt and breeches torn, soaked to the skin, covered in mud. He said the Thames had broken in. He'd been inspecting the workings – his huge bulk making it specially difficult for him – when quicksands were encountered. They burst in with such an onrush of water that, as they all raced back, stumbling through the low, narrow bore nearly a quarter of a mile long by now, it had risen above their shoulders, necks, chins, and was within inches of the roof before they were swept into the shaft and washed up to the surface.

Amazingly no one had been drowned. But being so close to success, Richard was quite undaunted. He immediately had the hole on the river-bed plugged with a vast quantity of clay; and had totally drained the entire length of the tunnel within days. By 2 February, only a week after the disaster, he was able to tell Giddy that the men were back at work and he expected to bring the bore to the surface on the north bank in ten or twelve days time at most.

This time it was the company, not Trevithick, that gave up. They could not believe their engineer could really overcome this catastrophe. Some had no faith in him anyway; they had had a grudge against him ever since Vazie was forced out. And when the Lord Mayor of London protested at the river-bed of the Thames being interfered with by having all that clay pushed into it, they ordered work to cease while they thought it through.

Richard was astonished. Some of them had wanted him to expand the bore into a full-size tunnel when he was only halfway through. Because he had advised against this, they had considered him incompetent. Now even those who believed in him talked of bringing in outsiders to assess his ability. He showed them that, if they were worried by further flooding, the job could be done by lowering caissons. Pump out the water from them and they would serve as coffer dams in which men could lay cast-iron tubing to form the tunnel. But they were not impressed.

By this time Richard had engaged an engineer to assist him called John Rastrick whose father, a Northumbrian millwright, had built many of Trevithick's engines at a works he had set up among the iron foundries of the Black Country. Though fully committed to helping drive the tunnel, young Rastrick was sorry nothing more had been heard of Trevithick's locomotives since their successes in Wales and on Tyneside.

Jane, meanwhile, hated everything to do with the tunnel. It had not only forced her to live in this stinking place on the Thames but had also nearly drowned her husband. She must have longed for him to get back to the work she knew he was most cut out for. And with John Rastrick clearly feeling much the same, even suggesting his father's firm could build whatever new locomotive he designed, and with Richard himself so insulted by having other engineers called in to report on his competence. . . . However reluctant he might have been to admit it, he fully understood what they were saying.

It was a sombre Robert Stevenson who returned to the Bell Rock that April. He found the wooden beacon in such good order that some nails left by the smith were still lying just where they had fallen; even the ashes of his last fire were undisturbed. But everywhere were droppings from the seagulls and cormorants who had evidently made full use of the place; and in the big shallow pool made by the partly excavated pit for the lighthouse foundations crabs and limpets had made their home. He could be forgiven for thinking that nature would always win in the end.

He had good cause to be so depressed. Less than a month after Christmas his twins, debilitated by measles and then whooping cough, had both died. His daughter Janet was then so ill that he and his wife 'could only look forward mournfully', and within a fortnight she too had died. He took comfort from the fact that his two remaining children, Jane aged seven and the nine-month-old baby Alan, were both in good health, and in a letter to Rennie, who had written to him at length with his condolences, he stressed that 'since all these dispensations of Providence are wisely ordered, it becomes us in all things to submit to the will of God.'

His wife had become almost insensible with grief. It was weeks before he could even get her out of the house. Did she take any comfort from knowing she was already three months pregnant again? Robert would have done. And in his case he had his work to escape to. When Peter Logan and Francis Watt returned with the men, it was hard to believe from the energy he displayed that he had suffered any such tragedy at all.

That their own lives hung on a thread had been brought home to him when they all came so near to drowning during the great gale. Because the *Pharos* was indeed just a Floating Light, to be tossed about like a cork wherever the wind blew, he had decided to work instead from a proper ship that at least had the sail power to escape from a storm. Named after the man who persuaded the Board of Trade in London to give its backing to the lighthouse, the *Sir Joseph Banks* was a schooner that had been built for him, now fully fitted out and about to join them off the rock.

Since the beacon had a platform that the waves could never reach, it was no longer necessary every two hours when the tide came in to make for the boats. At the moment Logan gave the word – always he had to keep an eye on the craftily advancing sea – the men hacking out the foundation pit would drop their picks and retreat to the deck of the beacon. Here they would set about helping Francis Watt's joiners before the tide went down again and they could get back to the pit.

Since it was always full of water when they returned to it, at least half an hour was spent on every visit just baling it out. Although it would mean even more time baling, Robert told them it must be a lot deeper yet – another 14 inches to be hacked out over the whole area.

Sharpening their picks at his forge kept James Dove constantly employed. But once the foundation pit had been fully excavated picks would no longer be needed. So expecting to be back home soon in Brechin, he'd have been astonished to hear he was not only wanted for a long while yet, but that Robert had arranged for another smith to join him to help him forge all the ironwork needed to lay a railway.

Robert had anticipated the arrival of the first stones. In the previous autumn he had conducted a trial, unloading a single ton-weight block from the *Smeaton* into one of the purpose-built praams and successfully landing it. It had worked well, but to get these stones from their landing stages to the site meant manhandling them over very jagged rocks. There would be a danger every second they could be dropped. And once chipped, they'd be no use at all. So he had decided to carry them in wagons on a railway, to run level all the way to the site, through specially hacked out cuttings and across bridges over chasms. All the necessary iron would be shipped out to the forges for the smiths to beat into the lengths and shapes required.

Even though the beacon house had no sides yet, it was already becoming much more than an emergency refuge. Many men preferred to sleep here on the open platform than have nights at sea on the *Sir Joseph Banks*. Dove, for instance, would sleep beside his anvil every night and get on with his work as soon as he woke. Food and drink were always left here for those who wanted to stay.

With extra men now engaged to make up for time lost by baling, and more joiners working on the wooden beacon house, an extraordinary scene presented itself. As Robert later recorded, 'the surface of the rock being crowded with men and the two forges flaming, one above the other on the beacon from which volumes of smoke ascended, gave the whole a most fanciful appearance, the noise of the picks and thunder of the anvils rebounding against the clamour of the surging seas.'

To take advantage of every low tide, torches were lit so that men could work at night. One night, as they were about to row back to the schooner, Robert told

Rennie 'the ebb had little sea, but with the flood it got up all at once as a thick fog came on. I got all mustered to the boats but by the time we could get off, the waves on both sides, from south and north, were meeting while we escaped between them – to be sometimes lifted up and suddenly let down. It was midnight, and thick weather. Each boat has a compass and blowing horn, and the schooner a bell and half a dozen horns by which means we can find our way in fog. You can conceive what noise it makes when nine horns and a large bell meet in clangour.'

At night the fires from the forges, and the torches lit on the worksites, made the rock look to distant ships, as one sea captain reported, like an erupting volcano. Even by day, said Robert, 'such columns of smoke ascended we were often mistaken at a distance for a ship on fire.'

By 7 July the foundation pit, a perfect circle 42 ft across and several ft deep, was ready at last to receive the first stones. At the workyard in Arbroath the masons from Aberdeen had long since cut them. Each one had fitted exactly into the appropriate wooden mould for it that James Slight had made from the pattern. And in the centre of the yard, on a huge round platform the same size as the base of the lighthouse, this first course of stones, to cover the entire foundation area, had been laid out, loosely dove-tailed together for inspection by Robert.

Once approved, it was set aside for shipment and the next course prepared and laid out for inspection the same way. Every day now the rough-hewn blocks from the quarries were being delivered one by one from the harbour on the sling–cart. To the people of Arbroath, the indefatigable horse, Bassey, led by its minder, James Craw, plodding slowly along the cobbles of the Ladyloan with its huge heavy stone was already a very familiar sight.

On 9 July the horse made its first return journey with a finished product – the foundation stone. Transported to the rock by the *Smeaton*, it was lowered onto a praam and brought ashore. Decorated for the occasion, it was carried to the site and placed in position in the centre of the pit, as Robert led the prayer – 'May the Great Architect of the universe complete and bless this building.'

Working as masons now, the men began to lay the foundation floor. The stones for it arrived regularly, to be loaded into praams for carrying to the landing stages. Although the railway had not yet been built and they had to be manhandled to the site, there were no mishaps. Soon all 123 blocks of the first course, covering the entire floor of the foundation pit, had been laid and trenailed together.

The second course was laid in only seven sessions which, allowing for the time spent baling out, meant the job was done in under twelve hours. The next course presented more difficulties, but each time a layer was laid the pit became shallower till after the fourth course it had been filled altogether with much cheering from the men that there was no more baling out to do. But with the weather now worsening, work had to cease for the winter.

Just over two months earlier a curious announcement had appeared in *The Times*. It stated:

> We are credibly informed that there is a Steam Engine now preparing to run against any mare, horse or gelding that may be produced at the next October Meeting at Newmarket. The wagers at present are stated to be £10,000, and the engine is the favourite. Trevithick, the patentee, has been applied to by several distinguished personages to exhibit this engine to the public prior to its being sent to Newmarket. We have heard that its greatest speed will be 20 miles in one hour, and its slowest never less than 15 miles.

A few days later it was announced in *The Observer*:

> The most astonishing machine ever invented is a steam engine with four wheels, so constructed she will with ease and without any other aid gallop from 15 to 20 miles an hour on any circle. She weighs 8 tons and is matched for the

An attraction in Bloomsbury – train rides on Trevithick's Catch-Me-Who-Can locomotive.

next Newmarket meeting against three horses to run 24 hours starting the same time. She is now in training on Lady Southampton's estate adjoining the New Road near Bedford Nursery. We understand she will be exposed for public inspection on Tuesday next.

Although still hoping to convince the Thames Archway Company that he could complete the tunnel in the way he had proposed, Richard had finally agreed to resume work on his locomotive. John Rastrick, through his father's firm, had taken on the job of building it to Richard's design, and it was soon on the way to London.

Just why London had been selected for the trials is a mystery. Was it Davies Giddy's idea? Even more influential since becoming engaged to the daughter of Lord Gilbert in Eastbourne, he might well have thought that in London it could be brought to the attention of potential backers more easily than by showing it off in such remote regions as south Wales or Tyneside. But whose idea was it to promote it with a publicity stunt that would have done credit to a PR firm of the 1990s? Certainly not Richard Trevithick's. Even the staid, academic Giddy is unlikely to have thought it up. But he had an adventurous married sister, Mrs Guillemard, who was bold enough to be one of the first to travel on the train when it ran and invented the teasing name for it 'Catch Me Who Can'. She had money of her own from estates she had inherited, was married to a close friend of her brother's, John Guillemard – like Giddy, a Fellow of the Royal Society – and living as they did at 27 Gower Street, where her brother sometimes stayed when in London, her house looked straight onto the land which was leased to them for the staging of the trials.

Certainly it was a brilliant stunt. First tell the press that some kind of bet has been arranged: news of a contest with large sums of money staked on the outcome can be guaranteed to excite the public. No evidence exists that bets were in fact made at all, or even that a race between the engine and horses at Newmarket was ever seriously intended; it certainly never took place. It was the publicity alone that mattered. When Samuel Homfray in Wales read the story in *The Times* he wrote at once for details as he wanted to bet on it himself.

Once the necessary land had been leased, someone at least, if not Mrs Guillemard, had the clever idea of erecting a tall fence round the circular track so that no one could see what was happening inside. The sight of smoke puffing into the air from the noisy machine parading unseen behind the fence would soon draw the crowds. They would eagerly pay a shilling a head to come in just to satisfy their curiosity. Their tickets entitled them not just to admission, but to ride behind the engine in a carriage if, like Mrs Guillemard, they so dared.

Richard was determined that this time nothing should go wrong. As his letters to Davies Giddy, nowadays spending most of his time with his bride-to-be in Eastbourne, reveal, he took the greatest trouble to ensure that the circular track he laid down would support the weight of the locomotive. He laid timber under the iron rails, embedded it deeply in the earth, and after many hours spent pushing the engine around by hand, taking up the rails and relaying them wherever they were found to have dipped, he was finally ready to let in the public.

It was just about then that he heard from the Thames Archway Company that, despite all his proposals for completing the tunnel, they intended to abandon the project altogether and pay him off. The most he would get for three years of work and the brilliance of his ideas was £500.

So his future career now depended once more on the interest he could arouse with his locomotive. Catch me who can? Who was even going to try?

CHAPTER FIVE

The Light Shines Out

By now, August 1808, the war with France had been going on, apart from one brief truce, for fifteen years. It did not seem to affect the flamboyant social life of the land-owning upper classes on whose behalf it was being fought. In the country houses the balls went on as usual; in the London season fashionable society paraded itself in Vauxhall Gardens and the Mall, and at Covent Garden and Drury Lane Theatres. Few cared what Napoleon was up to on the continent. The fact that Sir John Moore had just been sent with 10,000 men to strengthen the British position in the Spanish Peninsula was only of concern to most people when they heard of his death at Corunna and the full retreat of his bedraggled troops.

It was the businessmen, the merchants, bankers and industrialists who cared most about the progress of the war. Not that they cared much who won it. They might even have secretly agreed with young intellectuals like William Hazlitt that the French Revolution would never have resorted to the Terror of the guillotine if foreigners had not intervened. As it was, the ruling classes in the rest of Europe had been so scared that such rebellion might happen to them that together their countries had attacked France on all her borders to try to restore the *ancien régime*.

The City of London might also have agreed that some of Napoleon's social reforms would be of benefit to England too, though any suggestion that the common people had the same right to clamour for Liberty and Equality would, of course, have appalled them. But to have the French emperor lampooned as such an ogre that children could be disciplined by warning them that Boney would get them if they misbehaved was probably seen by them as just a ploy by Pitt's government to stay in power.

The Whigs wanted peace at any price which is why they had big business behind them. For fifteen years expanding industries like the cotton mills of Lancashire had been cut off from their customers on the continent. Who cared who ruled Europe as long as it could be turned into a market once again for British goods? At least the battle of Trafalgar had given Britain command of the sea once again; and with young General Wellesley's success in driving out the French from India, there was hardly a country in the world now that British manufacturers could not turn to for any imports they needed, and at their own price too. And with rival industries on the continent virtually destroyed by the ravages of the Napoleonic wars, they had no competition.

The foppish Prince of Wales might not have known it, nor the fashionable society of London or Bath, nor the landscape artists, or architects now giving the capital such elegant squares and terraces, nor the poets like Wordsworth and Coleridge, and romantic novelists like Sir Walter Scott, but in fact the stage was now set to make Britain into the most powerful commercial and industrial nation on earth.

Men like John Rennie might have known it. They provided the infrastructure on which it would all depend – docks, canals, roads, bridges. Indeed they were so sure of themselves, so confident that once Napoleon had been seen off Europe would be cleared for business and there'd be nothing to stop them, that they had no need to experiment at all with such way-out ideas as steam locomotives.

Steam had its uses in factories, and for driving machinery generally; but on the roads and canals horse power was more than adequate, and ships did well enough at sea by harnessing the wind. So what was the point of this smoking contraption running round in circles on a field in Bloomsbury?

There was no doubt it was entertaining. Hundreds of people turned up to pay their shillings and thrill to the sight of it careering around so noisily with its laughing invitation on the front to try to catch it. To ride in the carriage behind it, like Mrs Guillemard, was added fun. And as a spectacle it matched one of the aquatic displays at Sadlers Wells theatre or an equestrian performance at Astley's.

Did even its inventor see any more in it? After three months drawing the crowds, shillings enough had been taken to pay for the running costs but no serious investor had come forward. So after a night of heavy rain, which softened the ground to cause a dip under the curved track that sent the locomotive flying off the rails, Richard Trevithick could do no more than pick up the pieces and close down his stall for good.

As usual he was not downhearted. He never had been able to envisage any real future for steam locomotion anyway. He had once had the idea that ships could be driven by steam too but could see no future in that either. Sir Samuel Bentham, Director of Naval Works at the royal dockyards, had asked him to build an engine that might drive a fireship into the harbour at Boulogne to destroy the French invasion barges there. Richard had set about the challenge enthusiastically. But he asked Davies Giddy not to mention it to his wife in case he had to be on board himself to set the fireship in motion to make sure it blew up among the enemy shipping at just the right moment. Fortunately, Napoleon abandoned his invasion plans before the project got further advanced.

What Richard had had in mind was an engine with a crankshaft laid across the beam of the vessel with a paddle-wheel each end of it. He had already proved it was possible. On hearing that an engine of his was to be taken by horse-drawn barge to a mill in Macclesfield, he had had it fitted with paddle-wheels and started up just to see if it could drive the barge itself. It did the job so well it went at 7 mph. So he then adapted in the same way a passenger boat that sailed on the Broads between Yarmouth and Norwich. Its owner was delighted to report that sometimes the paddle-wheels propelled it at almost 12 mph. Yet Richard never even went there to see it in action. Even when several years later he came up with a patent for a screw-propeller to drive ships, he did not hang around to see if it worked.

In 1809 he was far more interested in a patent he had just taken out with a new business partner, Robert Dickinson, which he was sure would make their fortune. It was for iron tanks to be used for the carrying of cargo in ships' holds. Being so much thinner than wooden containers, they would take up far less room; and could also be used to carry water as ballast instead of the gravel that with much expense of labour was normally taken on board.

They had other uses too – in salvage, for instance. It was with the aid of his tanks he took on a job to raise a sunken ship off Margate. Filled with water they were lowered onto the wreck and fixed to it, and once the water had been pumped out to be replaced by air, they became buoyancy chambers. With the wreck now brought to the surface and ready to be towed home, it was typical of Richard that he had not yet agreed a price for the contract. Seeing the job was already as good as done, the client named a figure that Richard thought derisory. But instead of using the power he had just then to get whatever price he wanted, he simply ordered his men to detach his tanks and let the wreck drop back onto the bottom again.

His wife had a much shrewder head for business, and she suspected that Dickinson was cheating them. But her husband would have nothing said against his new partner, and although he could see for himself they were getting heavily into debt, he was sure his iron tanks would easily repair their fortunes – till one day the bailiffs were at his door and he was carried off to a debtors' prison.

It was a man called Henry Maudslay who baled him out, by buying the tank patent from him for far more than it was really worth. To slip into his life and out again with barely a word of thanks from anyone was typical of Maudslay. As will be seen, he played a very big part behind the scenes in the saga of the pioneering engineers.

Though free from the creditors who had had him locked up, Richard was at a low ebb after his experience in prison, and was now suddenly taken ill with typhus. Complications set in. Gastric fever turned to brain fever. Jane was distraught. Dickinson's doctor said one thing, Giddy's another. Once when she was convinced he was dying, she ran out into the streets to get help from the first man she met.

Although three months later he was at last out of danger, he was a shadow of his former self. The giant who could once throw a sledge hammer over a house was so weak he could hardly stand. It was imperative they got him back to Cornwall. But he was in no state to travel on the coach and they just didn't have the money to book a passage for them all by sea. So Jane went home with her three youngest by road, leaving her eldest boy, aged eleven, to accompany his sick father on the ship.

It was an eventful voyage. They had just passed Dover when they were spotted by a French man-of-war. It gave chase, but fortunately their ship, which regularly sailed this coast and knew it better than the French, put on sail and escaped its pursuers. Six days after leaving London it tied up in Falmouth harbour from where it was sixteen miles to the family home in Camborne – not the house where

Trevithick's mother's house at Penyponds, to which he returned destitute in 1810.

they had lived in happier days, which Richard had sold on their coming to London, but the small thatched cottage at Penyponds where he had been brought up as a child.

By now he knew that, while he was so ill in London, his aged mother had died. They had kept the news from him till he recovered. His son recalled how, on nearing the cottage, his father took his hand to lead him up the path to the front door. Jane and the rest of the family greeted them. Life would start again where for Richard it had started before.

As his strength returned, he became more and more optimistic about the future, although Jane suspected that during the six months of Richard's illness Dickinson had been feathering his own nest at their expense. So it may not have come as a surprise to her when her husband was declared a bankrupt.

And it probably did not surprise her either that, though Richard now had nothing but the house where he was born, he set about obtaining work from the local mines in just the same way he had done when in his teens, and with the same energy and determination to succeed.

In Scotland, the winter of 1808/9 had been so bad that work on Bell Rock could not resume till May, and even then it was still snowing. Earlier Robert had sent the *Smeaton* up the Tay to fetch more granite from a quarry. It encountered such dangerous ice floes it was nearly wrecked. On 1 June from his cabin on the *Sir Joseph Banks*, Robert wrote about a gale that made most men prefer to spend their nights on the unfinished beacon house than endure the horrors of the tossing ship.

'Amid the hissing of the winds and creaking of the bulkheads,' he said, 'rolling and pitching as we were, I spent the night reflecting on how they were faring on the beacon. As soon as a boat could approach, I sent cooked provisions and a kettle of mulled wine to the prisoners; they'd gone 30 hours without proper diet while exposed both to the winds and the sprays.'

Apparently it was James Glen, the ex-seaman joiner, who had kept up everyone's spirits – by vividly describing to them such dreadful experiences he claimed to have endured at sea that by comparison 'their state on the beacon,' as Robert put it, 'was one of comfort and happiness.' When their food ran out, Glen said he was once on a ship where they had nothing to eat but the rats they could catch. 'By such means,' wrote Robert, 'he managed to cheer up the forlorn party.'

Soon the railway was finished. It ran direct from the landing stages to the site where it circled the base of the tower. From there each stone it carried could be raised to its position by the crane that stood on the workings. Knowing the time would come when the centre of the tower would be hollow, leaving the crane shut in by the thick walls rising around it, Robert and Francis Watt devised what was called a balance crane – a horizontal gib that could move up a vertical column through its centre, one end weighted to counterbalance whatever load was lifted by the other.

There were major problems. Not enough granite was reaching the masons; so for the upper part of the tower, Robert had to resort to sandstone instead. He was a stern taskmaster. He bawled out the captain of the *Smeaton* for not having checked, after a gale, if the lightship might have needed assistance. The mate of the *Sir Joseph Banks* was ordered to explain why a praam had been lost and in the same letter why a bell wasn't rung for Sunday service. And when there appeared on a pay roll two seamen's names that Robert didn't recognise he instantly wanted to know on whose authority they'd been taken on, and what for. Nothing escaped him.

The terrible weather continued. There were such high seas that, even at low tide, breakers would come charging in to drench a newly-laid course of stones and wash away the mortar in them before it had had time to set. So fresh supplies were constantly being called for by the mortar mixers, a new group of men now working beside the smiths on the beacon house and getting as irritated by the smoke in their eyes from the forges as their own lime fumes got up the noses of the smiths.

Several rooms had now been added to the beacon house, a dormitory for the men, an office, cabins for Robert and Logan, and a galley ruled over by a popular new cook as much revered for his knowledge of medicine – in a varied career he'd been a soldier, valet, clerk and apothecary – as for his skill in the kitchen.

Steadily the tower grew taller, a solid mass of stone which finally topped the level of the highest tide. No longer could the sea wash over their work. To celebrate its final banishment, there was a special issue of grog, loud cheers from the men, flags hoisted and prayers led by Robert to give thanks to the Builder of the Universe. Soon the rock was so tamed that work could go on quite regardless of what the sea was up to. A ropeway extended from the beacon to the tower so that men and materials could move freely between the two at all times.

There had been accidents. The previous year a boy had drowned as he tried to fix a hawser from the *Smeaton* to its mooring. Caught by a wave, he had been swept away within seconds. His widowed mother was distraught. What he earned was her only income. But she had another son, little more than a child. So Robert took him on in his dead brother's place so his mother would not lose money by it. She was ever so grateful.

Fog would descend almost without warning. One evening some men rowing to their ship became so enwrapped in it they lost their way and found themselves far out to sea when it cleared. It was sixteen hours before they got back; they had rowed all the time without food or water. They were so debilitated they could barely stand.

And now a worker called Wishart was injured. This burly man had been standing under the crane when the jib got released by mistake and fell on him. He

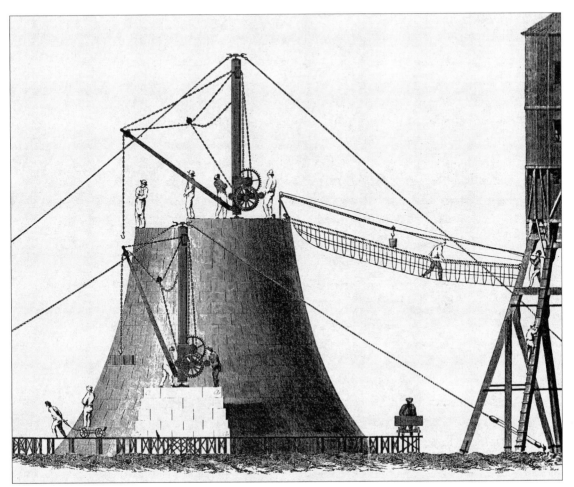

The beacon house linked to the site by a ropeway, so work could go on regardless of the tide. From the railway round the tower stones were hoisted by crane to their positions; later, when the ropeway was made into a solid bridge, they were raised direct from the praams so no time was lost even when the railway was under water.

wasn't killed, but his legs were smashed; and by the time they got him back to Arbroath, he was in a very bad way. Robert paid for a nurse to attend him and was pleased to learn his legs would not have to be amputated and that 'there is daily less to be apprehended from their mortification'.

Wishart was just twenty-five. In December he wrote to Robert to tell him:

> . . . I have got my foot almost sound, and am inteinding to go home in a month or tow, and as I am no great scolar I will go to school and hope you will not have an objection. Whether I be fit for work, I am doubtfull. In consideration of

which I have been thinking if I could get in for a gauger, if you would make any intrest for me. But indeed sir you have been so kind to me I cannot but give you a thousand thanks for what you have done for me. It has been a Great Misfortune but it was the works of providence and why should I complain while I am alive. Sir, if you would be so good as to give me a few lines somewhere when you receive this . . .

In August the building was 17 ft above high water. Its very presence, standing defiantly in the path of the winds, got in their way so much that they hit back with tremendous force. In his cabin in the beacon house Robert watched seas sweeping up to drench the masons on the tower and infuriate the mortar-men 'for the diluting effect on their carefully prepared cements.' But he knew for sure now that the rock which had terrorised mariners for centuries had been rendered powerless, and that the dream he had had over ten years ago would inevitably come true.

When work ceased that autumn, the men sailed back to Arbroath to a tremendous ovation from the townsfolk. Robert wrote that the *Smeaton:*

. . . being decorated with our colours and having fired a salute on approaching the harbour, a multitude assembled on the quays to greet us. Having made good wages, the men spent the evening with innocent mirth and jollity. Always they had gone to their arduous task cheering, and always returned in the same hearty state. At the rock, between tides, they had amused themselves reading, fishing, playing music or cards, or in sporting with one another. In the workyard at Arbroath the youngest were almost without exception employed in the evening at school; not a few learning architectural drawing, for which in a very obliging manner they were assisted by Mr Logan, Clerk of the Works.

Robert spent much of the winter working on the light that would shine out when the house was completed. To distinguish it from others, he designed it to show alternately white and red, an effect achieved by rotating round the lamps the different coloured panes of glass and opaque substances between them. The apparatus, and clockwork machinery to drive it, was to be made in Edinburgh by Thomas Smith's firm at Greenside, just behind the family house in Baxters Place, together with the lamps. The entire lightroom would then be shipped to the rock and assembled on the tower.

By now Robert had had another son, born in August 1808. Most of the children tended to be born in July or August – Robert was nearly always at home in good time for Christmas. True to form, when he returned to the rock in the spring of 1810 he knew that his wife would be giving birth again in July. It was to be another boy, though two years later he too was to die in infancy.

In view of what happened to so many of her children, it was as well that Jeannie had her strong religious faith to live by. Together with her spinster sister Janet, now twenty-seven, she did not merely seek comfort through her prayers; she started a school for homeless orphans that met regularly at their home in Baxters Place. Did her redoubtable mother-in-law, Jean, now sixty, help with it? Her father, Thomas Smith, would surely have kept well out of the way. He had retired by now, leaving the lighting business to his son. Not that he seems to have liked James all that much. In a letter to Robert in 1810 he grudgingly stated that at least 'James is becoming more attractive in his habits'.

Thomas died in 1815. A year later his one remaining unmarried daughter, Janet, then thirty-two, married James's business partner. James himself died at the young age of thirty-seven, and it seems ironic that of all Thomas Smith's progeny it was the most other-worldly of them all who became in the end the one member of his family to be involved, albeit only by marriage, in the business he had made into such a success.

In 1810 when work resumed on the rock, Robert had the ropeway to the tower from the beacon converted into a firm wooden bridge. He then set a crane on it so that stones could be raised direct from the praams to be wheeled along the bridge to the site. The railway and landing stages had ever only been available at low tide. Now they could be dispensed with altogether.

With the solid base of the lighthouse completed, all subsequent courses to be laid merely circled the space for the interior. But the walls still had to be immensely strong, able to resist wind pressure up to 5 tons per square foot. Nearly 6 ft thick above the solid base, they gradually dwindled to only 3 ft at the top. But by 7 June the 39th course had been laid; and just one week later, the 47th. On that day Robert wrote to his wife to tell her of the safety measures he had introduced, aware that as the tower grew taller it also got narrower and gave less and less room for the men to work at these dangerous heights. Elsewhere he recorded that 'waves of considerable magnitude sweep like lightning up the sloping sides of the building to drench men working over 60 feet above the rock'. He saw sprays that 'fell in the most wonderful cascades down the walls of the building in froth as white as snow, producing a kind of drift that rose 30 ft in height like a fine downy mist which fell upon the face and hands more like a dry powder than a liquid substance. The effect of these seas as they raged among the beams of the beacon house and dashed upon its higher parts produced a tremulous motion which to a stranger must have been frightful.'

It must have been frightful enough even to those who were used to it, though the typically terse Robert would never have admitted that. By now everyone was living in the beacon house, the men so cramped in their dormitory that their bunks were arrayed on five tiers with only eighteen inches between them. They knew their home was supported over the sea only by the six timbers they had put up three years ago. One night it seemed these wooden stilts couldn't possibly stand up to a gale that smashed waves against them of such ferocity that the whole place shook with what Robert called 'tremulous motion'.

Next morning the floor of the smiths' platform had been swept clean of everything on it. The cast-iron tubs the mortar men used, the iron hearth of the forge, the smiths' bellows, even their anvils, all were found at the next low tide scattered on the rock many yards away.

In Arbroath the stone cutters knew that very soon now they would be laid off. Already James Craw and his stalwart horse Bassey had been taken on board the *Smeaton* which was to bear them to Leith, where they came from, so that they could carry, from workshop to port, the stones prepared there for the cornice and parapet of the lightroom.

On the way the ship called at the rock, and when a sudden fog came on it was very nearly wrecked, its master only realising how close to danger he was by the sound of the smith's anvil from the nearby beacon house. What James Craw must have felt has never been recorded, let alone the feelings of the horse.

In Leith, the time soon came when Bassey and Craw made their last journey with a stone – the one that was to be placed in the middle of the very top course of the tower to support the pre-fabricated lightroom to be assembled upon it. To celebrate, both Bassey and Craw were garlanded with ribbons. Together they had carried, one by one, each of the 2,835 separate stones that had now been turned into the Bell Rock lighthouse.

Incidentally, the horse, which according to the accounts had cost the Northern Lighthouse Board £25 to buy and £56 a year to feed, ended its days in dignified retirement on the isle of Inchkeith, its skeleton bequeathed to the College of Surgeons at Edinburgh for the study of anatomy. Later it was passed to St Andrews University who put it in their Natural History museum. It is still there today.

As for the men who cut all the stones it carried, it had no sooner left them than they had a farewell party in the yard for which Robert gave David Logan, his

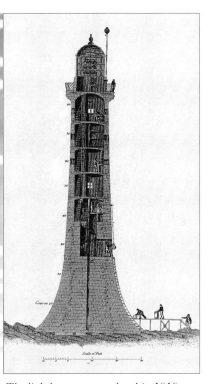

The lighthouse as completed in 1810.

In modern times it is as strong as ever, needing only to be checked out twice a year. Here the helicopter pad on the rock is about to be overflowed by the surging, incoming tide.

Clerk of Works, the sum of five guineas to pay for what he called 'the finishing pint'. He noted in his journal that they 'had a merry meeting with their sweethearts and friends and concluded their labours with a dance. But the consideration of parting, of leaving a steady and regular employment to go in quest of work, was rather painful after being harmoniously lodged for years together. So their happiness on this occasion was not without alloy.'

The laying of the final stone on the tower was attended with usual ceremony, Robert praying that 'the great architect of the Universe under whose blessing this perilous work has prospered may preserve it as a guide to the mariner.'

All that remained was to assemble the lightroom and fit out the interior rooms beneath it. For this a completely different team was recruited – carpenters, decorators, plumbers, upholsterers – all of whom now took over the beacon house till finally their job was finished too, and the beacon house itself and its walkway to the tower could be dismantled.

An advertisement was issued to shipping that the light would shine out on 1 February. It had long been decided that the first keeper would be John Reid who for the last four years had been in charge of the light on the *Pharos*. His place on the lightship was now taken by Captain Wilson who, as landing master for Robert, had been responsible for getting the men to and fro between the ship and the rock.

On the night of 1 February 1811 he raised the ship's lanterns as usual and looked towards the lighthouse on the rock. Here its first keeper had lit the lamp, and was ready to set in motion the revolving apparatus of different coloured glass, designed by Robert, that would let it shine out, with the red and white alternate beams the advertisement had prescribed. On seeing it, Wilson gave the order to extinguish, after four years, the provisional lights of the *Pharos*.

From that moment on, with only the briefest accidental interruptions, the Bell Rock lighthouse has never ceased to send out its warning beams to ships, emitting them this very night just as Robert Stevenson intended them to nearly two hundred years ago.

CHAPTER SIX

A Canal in the Sky

In July 1808, soon after the laying of the lighthouse foundation stone, a ship passed the rock on its way to Sweden. On board was a man who would certainly have been interested to see all the activity going on, since he had once tried to land there himself when asked by the NLB to advise on what was needed. Bad weather had turned him back but he sent in a hefty bill for his fee. Rennie, who couldn't stand the man, told Robert that 'he has no originality of thought and all his life has built the little fame he has acquired on the knowledge of others'.

His name was Thomas Telford – on his way just then to Gothenberg, in answer to a request from the King of Sweden to build a canal from the Baltic to the North Sea that would allow their ships to duck out of having to pay tolls to the Danes every time they sailed through the Sound round Elsinore. Never having been to sea before, and understandably nervous of attacks by the marauding French, Telford insisted on being provided with a naval escort. The Swedish government wanted him so much they persuaded an English admiral, at that time in Gothenberg, to have a frigate sent to Leith to accompany Telford's ship. Even then the engineer was so anxious about what could happen at sea that for the few days' voyage he brought enough food and liquor with him to supply an army.

That Thomas Telford could name his own terms for any job offered to him was, of course, what irritated Rennie. Ten years earlier the most acclaimed engineer in Britain had been himself. But by 1808 that glory was passing to Telford. Another Scot of even more humble origins – the son of a shepherd in Eskdale – Telford had made such a name for himself he was now laying roads all over the Scottish Highlands, building canals, bridges and new harbours, and opening up a waterway through the whole length of the Great Glen to link the north Atlantic with the North Sea.

He was also a great reader, especially of Scottish literature. Had he lived a couple of generations later, he would have delighted in the works of Robert Louis

Stevenson – author of *Treasure Island* and the grandson of the man who built the Bell Rock lighthouse.

In his *Records of a Family of Engineers*, Robert Louis Stevenson says his grandfather was 'first and last an engineer, but not in the field of engines. He was above all things a projector of works in the face of nature, and a modifier of nature itself.'

In fact, that description applies more to men like Rennie and Telford. Rennie's great breakwater at Plymouth, like his huge docks and harbour works elsewhere, subdued and modified the power of the sea in ways that Robert's lighthouse was not even intended to. So historically Rennie's works are more important than something which may have been of immeasurable benefit to shipping in the North Sea, but only indirectly to anyone else. Nor is it really significant that the lighthouse has needed so little attention in all the years it has been working. Apart from the lightroom being sometimes replaced to keep up with changes in technology and its rooms rebuilt in 1964 to provide more comfortable living quarters for the lightkeepers, and in the 1980s the light being automated to dispense with lightkeepers altogether, the fact that no other changes have ever been made is not really surprising. Almost all the creations of the early engineers have lasted just as long.

What makes it important is the *way* it was built. In discussing his grandfather, Robert Louis Stevenson goes on to say that 'for the civil engineer, the complexity and fitfulness of nature are always before him. He has to deal with the unpredictable. His work not yet in being, he must foresee its influence . . . He must not only consider that which is but that which may be.'

He could have added that a lesser man would think such unpredictable forces of nature could never be mastered just by men wielding picks and shovels. Stevenson had to contend with seas that only revealed the worksite for two hours at a time, and with waves that could sweep a man off a building 70 ft above him and knock lumps of granite around weighing more than a ton as easily as tennis balls. Yet despite such odds stacked against him, he never doubted he would win.

And it is this that epitomises the character of all the engineers who created the man-made landscape we take for granted today. Though neither Rennie nor Telford ever had to risk their lives the way Robert and his men did every day, they shared his conviction that in dealing with the forces of nature nothing but nothing was impossible.

Like Robert Stevenson, Thomas Telford was also an only child who never knew his father. Born in a shepherd's croft in the lowland Scottish country near

Langholm, he was just three months old when his father, barely into his thirties, died. So that his widowed mother could go out to work, the child was often left for long periods with other people. This may explain the reliance on his own self-sufficiency that was to govern his whole life. But he enjoyed school and working out of doors in his spare time for local farmers to eke out his mother's meagre income. Widowed as she was, she was strongly supported by her own family, and it was through her nephew, steward to Sir James Johnstone of Westerhall, that Thomas became apprenticed to a stone-mason in Langholm.

Here he not only proved himself an apt pupil, soon to become a highly skilled craftsman, but also was befriended by a lonely old lady who had noticed his curiosity about books and gave him the run of her library. He was so excited by the literature she showed him that he was soon reading everything he could, mainly poetry. It meant so much to him he began writing poetry himself – and continued to do so all his life.

But his love of literature, matched only by his love of the countryside, did not blind him to the fact that it would be his skill as a stone-mason that would prove most useful to him. Pragmatic and ambitious, he also knew – just as John Rennie would too some four years later – that if you wanted to make a name for yourself, your only chance was in England.

He had set his heart on becoming an architect. It would satisfy both his artistic aspirations and the need he felt in him to put the skill he had acquired with his hands as a mason to good use. But unlike Rennie who had made himself some money by the time he broke away from his millwright's background in Dunbar to head south, Telford had not even the means to make the journey. Hearing from his cousin, the steward to the Johnstones of Westerhall, that his master wanted to send a horse to London and needed someone to get it there, he offered to ride it for him. Sir James thought highly of young Thomas anyway and willingly agreed.

So in January 1782, when Rennie was still completing his course at Edinburgh University

Thomas Telford.

and growing equally restless, when Robert Stevenson's mother had just met Thomas Smith, and when Richard Trevithick was still just a rebellious schoolboy, Thomas Telford, with his mason's tools in his pack, had set out from Eskdale on horseback to seek his fortune down south.

The old lady who had let him have the run of her library had given him an introduction to her brother in London, who in turn passed him on to Sir William Chambers, the architect then building Somerset House. Thomas was taken on at once and proved himself so quickly that he was soon promoted. But unlike the men he worked with, whom he largely despised for being content to be no more than wage slaves all their lives, Thomas made plans to set up in business on his own.

It was just then that Sir James Johnstone of Westerhall wanted to make some alterations to his house in Eskdale; and asked his brother in London to seek out Telford to do the job. William Pulteney, who had taken the surname of his wife, was not just heir to the Westerhall estate, but on his marriage had become the wealthiest commoner in England. He got on so well with Telford he not only commissioned from him the Westerhall work, but gave him other building jobs too. Soon Thomas was doing so well he could write in a letter home that he could afford three clean shirts every week and have his hair powdered every day.

In 1786 Pulteney became MP for Shrewsbury and decided to rebuild his castle there that had long since fallen into disrepair. He asked Thomas to take on the work. It was a huge commission that immediately made him, as Pulteney's protégé, a man to be reckoned with in Shrewsbury. Within a year Pulteney had him made County Surveyor. In that capacity Thomas, still seeing himself as an architect, restored public buildings, built the town's new gaol and found himself responsible for all the county's bridges.

The Severn and its tributary rivers were notorious for the way they tended to flood after heavy rain in the Welsh mountains; bridges were constantly being damaged and often washed away. During the next ten years Telford was to design and build over forty new ones. One of them he erected by throwing a span of cast-iron across the Severn so that there was no masonry in the water to be pounded by the river when in spate. Almost without his knowing it, he was on his way to becoming an engineer.

In 1791 he was approached by the directors of the Ellesmere Canal Company. Until now, the enormous supplies of coal and iron that the country had been blessed with were virtually wasted because of hopelessly inadequate transport facilities. Coal could usually be delivered up to some twenty miles from the pithead on a network of horsedrawn railways serving all the collieries in the district, but roads were so bad it could never be sent any further unless there was a port near enough for it to be carried round the coast by ship. James Watt's improved steam-engines might dramatically step up production in factories, but if the carriage price of the coal they consumed was almost as high as the coal itself, and the bigger output that resulted could still not be delivered beyond the nearest market town, such engines were hardly cost effective.

So when the network of canals that James Brindley had envisaged when he first started building them for the Duke of Bridgewater in the 1760s began to come into being, they soon did so much for the industries they served that the resulting profits had investors caught up in what became known as 'canal mania'. The Ellesmere company raised all the capital it needed within a mere eight hours.

What the company had in mind was to link the Mersey to the Dee at Chester and to the Severn at Shrewsbury, and thus bring all West Midlands industry within waterway reach of both Liverpool and Bristol. Two different routes had already been surveyed and there was argument about which to adopt. So they asked John Smeaton to recommend a capable engineer to advise them. He named his former pupil, William Jessop, now a highly experienced canal builder. After surveying the two routes himself, Jessop recommended the one through Wrexham.

He agreed to be their consultant engineer. But despite his national reputation he was such a modest, unassuming man, already overburdened by so many demands on his time, that the directors seem to have felt the need for someone less committed elsewhere, and perhaps of more dynamic personality, to be in overall charge. Who better than the 36-year-old Thomas Telford, thirteen years younger than Jessop, the energetic County Surveyor for Shropshire, right-hand man of Pulteney, and much liked by the local ironmasters and industrialists?

Telford had no experience of canal building so he fully understood that whatever ideas he had for the canal must always be subject to approval by Jessop. Nevertheless, he thoroughly enjoyed being responsible for such an immense undertaking; and aware of the prestige it would bring him, made sure his contract did not preclude him from taking on other work which was now more than ever offered him. Doubtless it was this that so irritated Rennie. But like Rennie, he had the same capacity to think on a grand scale. If Robert Louis Stevenson is right that modifying nature to serve man is what a civil engineer does, none fits that description more aptly than Thomas Telford.

For the Ellesmere Canal to reach the Severn at Shrewsbury it had to cross the river Dee at Pont Cysyllte in the Vale of Llangollen. This meant taking it down one side of the valley in a series of locks and up the other with the aid of some more.

Such locks, quite apart from the expense of building them, not only slow down the passage of a boat passing through them but need a constant supply of water to feed them; for as a barge descends, it takes a lockful of water down with it. For this reason Brindley made his canals follow natural contours whenever he could, however long the route their meandering course took. On the Ellesmere, however, to cross the valley at Pont Cysyllte there seemed no other way at all but locks – at least down to the level where a straightforward aqueduct could be built from one side to the other. Of course, locks could be dispensed with altogether if the canal could be carried straight across at the top, but that was hardly a viable proposition, at least not to most people. What, build an aqueduct 120 ft in the air from one side of a valley to another, a distance of 2,500 ft? It was as outrageous as Robert Stevenson's plan, ten years later, to build a lighthouse on a submerged rock. But Thomas Telford had just the same confidence it could be done.

Jessop had himself mentioned this as a possibility in his original survey, but knowing how much masonry would be needed to take the weight of such a waterway, had ruled it out on grounds of cost. But Telford had an answer to that. Nothing like so much support would be needed, he said, if the aqueduct were made of iron.

So when he heard that the company, convinced that locks were still the only practical way to cross the valley, was about to seek tenders from contractors for just that job, he made them cancel the advertisements, though he knew he had to prove that an iron aqueduct was feasible.

Luck once again was on his side. The engineer of another canal, being built from Shrewsbury to the Wrekin to serve nearby collieries, had died suddenly and Telford had been asked to take over. The canal had to cross the river Tern, and for this a normal stone aqueduct lined with clay had been planned. Telford now changed this to a cast-iron trough – if only to demonstrate that even with the weight of a canal in it far less strength was required to support it.

Never before had cast-iron been used in this way. But three months later, following Telford's lead, two other engineers were recommending cast-iron troughs for aqueducts as well. Jessop was convinced and once the company knew that, they were reassured. To keep the distance to be crossed by the trough as short as possible, it had been planned to build up on the gentle slopes of the southern side an enormous embankment extending 1,000 ft towards the river. But Telford now had such confidence in his iron waterway he reckoned he could carry it across the whole width of the valley. An embankment just as high would still be needed to receive it, but its length could be cut in half, thus vastly reducing the amount of earthworks needed while increasing the number of arches from eight to nineteen. The masonry contract was awarded to a Lancashire builder from Colne, James Varley, and in July 1795 the foundation stone was ceremoniously laid.

The work took over ten years. Telford himself was hardly ever there to see its progress; and Jessop was engaged too on other work, such as building the West India docks in London. But at Pont Cysyllte they had implicit faith in the man Telford had appointed as his Inspector of Works.

This was Matthew Davidson whom he'd known in Langholm when they were learning their trade as masons together. He had sent for him as soon as he became County Surveyor. Matthew worked with him on bridges, had his wife and children join him, and soon liked Shropshire so much that never again did he find a good word to say about his fellow countrymen in Scotland. At Pont Cysyllte he lived on the site with his family in a cottage Telford had specially built for them.

Another man he came to rely on as much was John Simpson, 'a treasury of talents' as he called him, who took over the building contract when it proved too much for the original contractor. He was to work for Telford from now on whenever he had the chance, as also would Matthew Davidson.

So too would William Hazledine. A local ironmaster, he hoped to get the contract to supply the iron trough. Telford wanted him to get it too. They were both Freemasons, members of the same Lodge, which may perhaps be significant. Tenders had already been invited and the biggest ironmaster of all, John Wilkinson, had put in a bid. With his foundry producing more iron than he could ever sell, and therefore a fervent advocate of the canal, he had seen the possibilities in Abraham Darby's iron bridge over the Severn, the first of its kind – at the town appropriately named Ironbridge today – and with an eye to business had encouraged Telford to design iron bridges too. No wonder he was as instrumental as Pulteney in getting Telford put in charge of the Ellesmere Canal. A lot of iron, he reckoned, would be needed for that.

But Telford was big enough now to do without him, though if Hazledine was to get the contract, he must somehow put in a bid a lot lower than Wilkinson's.

There was a way to do this. The ironwork would not be required for a long while yet, time enough for Hazledine to acquire some land on the very edge of the site where he could open a foundry. To give him time to do this, Thomas held up a decision on the tenders submitted till Hazledine's came in. It was way below the price of anyone else's since he had no transport costs to pay.

As a businessman Telford was no craftier than any other. But like the most successful of them, he always knew what he wanted and had an uncanny ability to obtain the devoted services of those who could most help him get it – whether it was the influential William Pulteney, whom he had charmed for life as soon as he first met him, or able lieutenants like Simpson, Davidson and Hazledine who would follow him wherever he led.

He was conceited. Although he knew Jessop had at least as much to do with engineering the great aqueduct as he had himself, he was in a position to take all the credit and usually did. But this had more to do with ambition than with vanity. Long before the aqueduct was finished it was being regarded as some new wonder of the world, and on the strength of that Telford was everywhere sought after. It must have infuriated Rennie to see the excitement caused in 1801 by Telford's proposal for a new London Bridge – to be built of iron in one single span allowing tall-masted ships to pass under an arch 65 ft above the river. That it would never be built was plain to anyone who could see how many offices, exchanges and coffee houses in the City would have to be demolished to make room for its immense approach road.

But it all added to Telford's reputation. Rennie found that the building of bridges, canals and harbour works that hitherto had largely gone to him were now offered to Telford too. In Liverpool they asked him to engineer a piped water supply system for the city; and thanks to Pulteney's influence, he was now commissioned to make a survey of the Scottish Highlands with a view to building proper roads there and cutting a canal to link the lochs of the Great Glen into a continuous waterway.

Yet still the aqueduct that had opened all these doors for him was not yet finished. But no wonder it was causing such a sensation. Carriages would draw up at Matthew Davidson's cottage bearing local gentry come to view the scene and have him explain what was going on. On the southern slope they could see hundreds of men with shovels and wheelbarrows piling up the colossal earthwork for the approach. Across the river at their feet they saw huge cut stones being manhandled over precarious wooden footbridges to be raised aloft to the masons and mortar men high on the scaffolding round the piers they were building. All the stone was being quarried from the valley itself and cut to shape in a yard beside the river. Nearby was Hazledine's foundry, its blast furnaces forging the twenty separate lengths of iron trough, each to be 5 ft deep and 12 ft wide, with the iron arches beneath them that would be embedded into the masonry of the piers. Just think of the noise where formerly the only sound was that of the river running happily along between tree-lined banks and it's easy to visualise the amazed faces of the visiting sightseers.

It typified in one small valley the vast changes to the country that Telford and Rennie had set in motion. In 1800 Rennie was designing bridges for Edinburgh and Boston while knowing that at that very time his bridges at Kelso and Wolseley were being built, his three major canals being dug, his improved Glasgow docks very nearly completed and work on his London docks now starting.

Telford was doing similar work – and finishing for the government his survey of the Scottish Highlands. This led to his recommendations being immediately adopted and himself appointed to engineer a work that over eighteen years would see him build 920 miles of new roads, replace ferry crossings with 1,200 new bridges, improve harbours and drive the great Caledonian Canal from Fort William to Inverness.

As soon as they could be spared from Pont Cysyllte, he sent for his trusted team. To engineer the canal, Jessop had been asked already; now Telford called in Hazledine to provide the iron work, Simpson to take charge of masonry, and of course Matthew Davidson. Never thinking he'd have to live in Scotland again, certainly not in the Highlands where he liked to pretend that if there were any true justice in the world there'd be no natives left there at all but the hangman and the Provost, he nevertheless answered the call to become Telford's principal resident engineer.

If the sightseers at Pont Cysyllte had been amazed by what they saw, they should have seen what was happening in the Highlands in 1805. The country was so rough that the only accommodation for masons and labourers were tents or crude turf huts. They were fed from makeshift mobile kitchens, while pack horses stumbled up the hillsides in the foulest weather to bring supplies and building materials that specially commissioned ships had unloaded on the nearest shores. Telford had divided his vast work site into different areas in which some contractors were at one time employing over a thousand men each.

The engineering itself had problems enough. To get sufficient depth for the entrance lock at Inverness it had to be sunk 400 yards out to sea where the mud was such it took almost a year to sink enough clay and rock into it to make a firm enough base for work to begin. At the other end the problem was reversed: here the first lock had to be excavated out of solid rock. It took ten more locks to bring the canal from there up to the level needed, and they all had to be big enough to take not a narrow boat or barge, but an ocean-going ship. They had to be over 90 yards long.

Nevertheless, it has to be said that, though costing nearly a million pounds, the Caledonian Canal never justified itself. By the time it was finished – not till 1822 – there was not so much need for it anyway, and soon it was found that some of the contractors had done such botched work, sometimes skimping it deliberately to keep within the price they'd agreed, that often the sides of the locks would fall in. By the 1840s it needed to be almost entirely rebuilt. But in the summer of 1808, when Telford was sailing past the Bell Rock on his way to build an even bigger canal in Sweden, he had such faith in his team and the contractors they engaged that only once a year would he even go and check how they were doing.

It was three years now since the battle of Trafalgar. It had given Britain command of the sea, but Thomas Telford on his six-day voyage to Gothenberg didn't know that. He was still very glad to have his naval escort; Napoleon remained their enemy. And with no end to the war in sight, the euphoria of fifteen years ago that had led to such massive investment in the engineering works that he and Rennie had instigated was now fading away. What was the point of giving the country a good transport system if it was still cut off from markets abroad? Canals and new docks continued to be built, but there wasn't the rush to invest in them that there had been. Many still in construction were hard pressed to find the funds to complete them.

The Ellesmere Canal was one of them. On the long stretch via Wrexham to Chester, difficulties had always been anticipated. To avoid a huge stairway of locks, Jessop had wanted a long tunnel. But this was ruled out on grounds of cost. Now, with no new money coming in, this section had to be abandoned altogether. And south of Pont Cysyllte it was soon found it could not be continued to Shrewsbury either. Only by extending a branch going east all the way up to Nantwich, where it could join another company's canal to Chester, could it connect with the northern section to the Mersey that had long since been finished and was now in use.

So on 26 November 1805 when 8,000 people gathered at Pont Cysyllte for the grand opening of the aqueduct, the canal it carried could never reach the Severn and only by a long detour even get to Chester and from there to the Mersey. The whole point of building it had been lost.

Nevertheless, such considerations did not dampen the enthusiasm of the crowd that day, as they stood on the little road bridge across the Dee and lined the hillsides on both banks. Before them stood the magnificent array of nineteen stone arches rising to 120 ft in the air where they carried from one side of the valley to another the iron road 1,000 ft long that was soon to be nicknamed the 'stream in the sky'.

When the first boats could be spotted moving in line ahead against the backdrop of the clouds, from one of them so high up came the sound of a brass band playing 'Rule Britannia'. Everyone joined in. It was the band of the Shropshire Volunteers seated in one of the barges, perhaps not even wanting to look down from such a height onto the scene below. The canal is just 7 ft wide, with a railing only on one side, beside the towpath. Once you leave the solid mass of the embankment, to sail out into the sky towards the far-off hill ahead, you cannot see at all what is holding you up.

In other boats that day, linked together and led along the towpath by the horse, were directors of the company in two of them and the engineers in another. At the rear were two empty barges that later on that day would make the return journey with cargoes of coal from the nearest colliery. As the procession

Telford's Pont Cysyllte aqueduct, a waterway of 19 arches 120 ft above the River Dee in the vale of Llangollen.

reached the other side, it was greeted by gunners of the Royal Artillery who marked the occasion with a fifteen-round salute that reverberated through the length of the valley.

From now on through the century almost all the great engineering feats were to be marked with similarly grand ceremony and displays of patriotic fervour, even if known to many at the time that, like the Pont Cysyllte aqueduct, they might not meet the need they were built for. It was the fact that they were built at all, structures that to anyone but the engineers seemed beyond imagination let alone accomplishment, that was celebrated. This uncritical adulation from a public that loved nothing better than an excuse for the pageantry their country could always stage so well was an expression of what would soon become that sense of superiority over the rest of the world which characterised the British spirit for the next hundred years.

When Telford came home in the winter of 1808/9, having surveyed for the Swedes the route he recommended for their Gotha Canal, he was ready to do for England what he had already started in Scotland – provide a properly planned network of trunk roads that, when combined with the canals, would give Britain the comprehensive transport system its burgeoning industrial power required. That is not to say he *consciously* set out on such a mission – his deceptively light-hearted manner and charm disguised no more than steely efficiency. But he had an instinctive understanding of his own crucial role in the transformation of Britain that had now begun.

With Ireland separated from the mother-country by sea, communication between the two depended mostly on the ships that plied between Holyhead and Dublin. But just to get to Holyhead was problem enough, cut off as it was from the mainland by the Menai Straits. Add the difficulties caused by the mountainous terrain of North Wales that had to be crossed too, and after the Irish uprising of 1798 it was a matter of considerable concern to Pitt's government in London to improve communications. So Telford was asked to see what could be done.

At first he just surveyed a route through the North Wales mountains that motorists use today without giving a thought to how it was built nearly 200 years ago in such a hostile environment. Five years later he engineered a road from Shrewsbury to Bangor and five years after that from Shrewsbury to London. The road from Carlisle to Edinburgh followed, and from Liverpool to London, besides a survey of the Great North Road which he reckoned he could shorten by thirty miles. Not for nothing would he be hailed as the Colossus of Roads.

Unlike Rennie who thought it demeaning for a civil engineer to concern himself with roads, Telford's experience in Scotland, where he had laid them with a scientific precision never attempted since the days of the Romans, had given him a vision of a country where people could travel on land as smoothly and reliably as goods were carried on the canals. In both cases it was the horse that provided the necessary energy, though Telford was not averse to the use of steam-driven carriages of the kind that Trevithick had pioneered to carry people on roads. It was the idea that steam power should be used to carry them on *railways* that seemed to him, and to John Rennie, so absurd.

Railways had their uses in linking production centres with local ports or canals, but since it had been found that even the heaviest loads, if distributed in a train of wagons running on rails, could be easily hauled on the level by a horse, no other power was needed – except when the railway had to run uphill when a stationary engine at the top could be used to wind a chain that would haul up the load till the horse could take it on again. Such chains could also be used to let the weight of a descending load haul a lesser one up on the other track. A steam locomotive would doubtless do the work a bit faster, but in the carrying of goods or raw materials journey time was not so very important anyway.

Almost no one could visualise steam-driven trains carrying *passengers*. Admittedly a train could carry far more people than the mere eight or nine a coach could manage, but unlike the train the coach was free to take its passengers direct to wherever they wanted to go, the argument put forward in favour of roads over railways by many governments today. In that sense Telford was far more ahead of his time than any of the early steam train pioneers.

He had the support not only of the coaching companies and turnpike trusts, but of the passengers too. It was only ever the long time a journey took and the constant jolting from the terrible surfaces that people objected to. Once roads began to be dramatically improved through Telford's engineering and the inventiveness of John Macadam in providing surfaces we still call macadamised today, and from which the word tarmac derives, journeys became not just comfortable but fast.

From Manchester to London, a ride that once took at least four days could soon be done in just over one. Long before the railways took over, roads were so good you could leave London by coach after breakfast and be in Brighton in time for lunch. By then stagecoaches had become so popular and profitable there were over 3,000 of them running all over the country.

*

A typically busy scene at the Elephant & Castle, south London, in 1826, as coaches for the Brighton road depart and arrive.

Back in 1814 when this process of opening up the country had barely begun, Richard Trevithick, now discharged from bankruptcy – his resolute wife doing most no doubt to get his affairs in order – had almost forgotten he had ever invented a locomotive. But he was as busy as ever. One of his latest patents was for a screw-propeller to drive a ship. But he'd just had it installed, with the engine to power it, in a specially built hull and was getting ready for its trials, when he suddenly lost interest – on receiving a visit from a man who'd come specially to Cornwall to seek him out.

He was a merchant from Peru, partner in a company that had acquired a derelict silver mine 14,000 ft up in the Andes. It had once been worked by the Incas but had had to be abandoned when it filled with water. Just think of the untapped silver that must still be lying there! With the aid of Trevithick's pumping engines, what untold riches might now be extracted!

Richard was so excited there was no more thought about steamship propulsion. He began at once borrowing money again to build engines for the Peruvian mines. He had them shipped out and even when he heard a year later that in the high altitudes of the Andes none of them worked properly, he was in no way discouraged. They just needed to be fixed. He would go out himself to sort it out. And to his wife's dismay, that is just what he did. Another son had been born three years ago; now Jane was pregnant yet again. But Richard assured her, as he said goodbye to them all on the quay at Penzance, that he would come home a very rich man.

In fact, it was to be another ten years before he came home at all. And for all that time his wife never even heard from him.

Just a couple of months before his engines had been loaded onto the ship for Peru, the young colliery mechanic he'd once met on Tyneside, George Stephenson, demonstrated a locomotive his employers had asked him to build for them.

By then the continuing war with France had brought about a soaring rise in the price of horses and fodder which made many a colliery owner think that perhaps on their tramways there was something to be said for using steam locomotives after all. In fact, three were already built and running before Stephenson completed his *Blucher*. Unfortunately, it was no more efficient than the others, often broke down and as usual played havoc with the rails it travelled on.

Unlike Trevithick, about to set sail just then in pursuit of yet another dream of fame and fortune, Stephenson's faith in locomotives never wavered. If rails buckled under the weight of his *Blucher*, there was only one thing to do – strengthen the rails. So in partnership with an ironmaster called William Losh who had already asked him to work for him, he set about devising cast-iron rails that would not give way under pressure. If Trevithick invented the locomotive, it was Stephenson out of all the engineers working in this field at the time who most believed in its future and therefore most deserves the title, Father of Railways.

After Napoleon's defeat at Waterloo in 1815 had brought an end at long last to the war, Rennie was asked to build a bridge across the Thames that was later named after the battle that had brought the victory. Little did he guess that before the end of the century in London the name Waterloo would be more associated with the railway terminus there than with his bridge. But then while he and Telford carried on staking out the land for their roads and canals, neither had any idea that a barely literate Northumbrian of thirty-three would soon achieve a fame as an engineer that would far outstrip their own.

CHAPTER SEVEN
Fathers and Sons

George Stephenson's father had been a colliery fireman. He shovelled coal into the stoke-hole of a winding or pumping engine. He earned ten shillings a week and was answerable to the man who worked the engine who was known as the plugman. At the age of seventeen his son George who, like Richard Trevithick, had done odd jobs about the mine till then, and shown much the same aptitude for understanding engines, got a job as a plugman himself at another pit – where shortly afterwards his father joined him to become his fireman.

Stephenson senior was too poor to send any of his six children to school, yet despite their impoverished and disadvantaged childhood they all did amazingly well in life. George was perhaps the most ambitious. Still in his teens, he persuaded his gaffer to let him have a go as brakesman on a winding engine. It was a highly responsible job which controlled the cage that took the miners down to the coal face. Since it was up to the brakesman to make sure it slowed to a gentle halt as it hit the bottom, the miners not surprisingly objected to a mere boy being entrusted with their safety. But George, whose ability to persuade others to believe in him was to mark his entire career, got the chance he wanted. He did the job so efficiently he was employed as a brakesman from then on and paid accordingly.

Knowing he must get himself an education if he was ever to advance any further, he persuaded a teacher in a nearby village to give him three nights a week tuition, at threepence a week, in the rudiments of basic arithmetic and in some idea of how to read and write. Beyond that his studies never took him far. He had no mind for academic learning and all his life resented the evidence of it in others. No wonder he got on so well with Richard Trevithick when he met him. Both of them had an intuitive understanding of mechanical engineering which amazed, and annoyed, those who had spent years of study trying to acquire it. But whereas Trevithick had Davies Giddy to act as his intellectual mentor, Stephenson had no one to turn to.

By now he had married. The first woman he proposed to had been madly in love with him, but her parents had grander ideas for their daughter than to ally her to an illiterate mechanic. Although Elizabeth Hindmarsh protested she would never marry anyone else, George, it seems, was not quite so enamoured for he very soon proposed to another girl. When she turned him down, he immediately asked her older sister instead who, at thirty-three, thought she was on the shelf and only too pleased to find she wasn't. She accepted George at once, had a son by him whom they called Robert and two years later a girl, Fanny. But Fanny died, and very soon after so did her mother, leaving George with a two-year-old boy to bring up on his own.

This was a tough time for him. Though earning good money as a brakesman, and supplementing it by making shoes and mending clocks in his spare time, he was also providing for his father who had been blinded in an accident at the mine and unable to work. Now he found himself called up for service in the army and the only way out of that was to pay for someone else to go instead. This took almost all his savings and though his sister Nell had already moved in to help look after his young son, he seriously thought of emigrating to America.

It was just then he got his big break. One of the company's pits was out of action because the pump that kept it clear of water had broken down and no one could mend it, except George who swore he could fix it. A mere brakesman? Eventually, after all the mechanics and engine-wrights had failed, they let him try. After three days taking it apart and rebuilding it, he had it working better than ever.

He was paid a mere £10 for his trouble, but news of his success had reached the top brass in the company who soon appointed him their engine-wright in charge of all the machinery in their pits. He was given a horse to ride from one to the other, and as long as he kept their own machines in order he was allowed to freelance for other collieries too without any reduction in his salary. So by 1814 when he was working on the *Blucher*, he had already established at the age of thirty-three a reputation on Tyneside as a leading engineer, earning enough to send his son to a private day school in Newcastle for the sons of gentlemen.

Poor Robert. To make up for his father having no education, he himself was to have enough for both of them. Almost as soon as he could walk he had been packed off to the village school and expected to come home each day and tell his father what he learnt. Often, if he was spotted by his father slipping out to play, he would be ordered back indoors to study his books. Now that he was eleven and enrolled in Dr Bruce's Academy in Newcastle, George gave him a donkey to get him there and back – which could also carry the books he was studying to explain to his father in the evenings. From his son, it is said, George learnt geometry and the basic principles of physics, as well as improving his ability to read and write.

It was typical of the age, certainly of the Victorian society that succeeded it, for a son to be expected to follow in his father's footsteps, the eldest at least. The proud suffix 'and Son' over a shop or business was far more common than merely the linked names of a couple of partners. Rennie's sons became engineers; so did Trevithick's son Francis; so did Robert Stevenson's Alan. With George Stephenson, however, there was more to it. He seems to have wanted to use his son to extend his own power and reputation by making up in education and style for his own deficiencies in both.

It put a big strain on Robert. A delicate child at the best of times, he had not been expected as a baby even to live very long. But though thin and wiry, he had his father's inner toughness and strength of character, qualities which in the end were to drive a wedge between them.

Meanwhile, far away in the south of England, the young son of another engineer had also just been enrolled at an expensive private school. At the age of eight, Isambard Brunel had been sent by his father to Dr Morell's boarding school in Hove where, unlike at all other schools at this time, there was no special emphasis on the Christian faith, no prefect system and no corporal punishment. Dr Morell taught classics, but put just as much emphasis on science and mathematics. Isambard's father was as determined as Robert's to make his son into an engineer and chose the school specially for this purpose, but it was not in any way to benefit himself.

Unlike George Stephenson who had a chip on his shoulder all his life about his thick Geordie accent and lack of learning, Marc Brunel was a highly educated, tubby little man who brimmed over with cheerful self-confidence and charm. A Frenchman from Normandy, he had been a cadet in the Navy before coming home to find his country gripped by the Revolution. A self-confessed royalist, and dangerously proud to be, he was soon a marked man who had to flee for his life – but not before falling in love with Sophia Kingdom, a sixteen-year-old English girl then staying with his cousins in Rouen. As he set sail from Le Havre for America after a tearful parting, he assumed she would soon get back to England.

But it was just then that Britain declared war and all the ports were sealed. Sophia was arrested and carted off to a makeshift prison where she spent nine months in danger every day of summary execution on the guillotine set up in the courtyard. Only when Robespierre fell from power and an immediate amnesty was ordered for all held prisoner under his regime was she suddenly freed. Even then it was months before she got home to England where her family could barely recognise her after what she'd been through.

Marc, meanwhile, had been doing well in North America. In Ontario, Canada, he had met up with a wealthy merchant who commissioned him to build a canal. Soon he became Chief Engineer to the growing little town of New York and built a cannon foundry on Long Island to help in its defence. His design for the Congress building in Washington won first prize in a competition – till the judges changed their minds on the grounds it would be far too expensive. Hardly surprising; he had based it on the Palace of Versailles which is why they had liked it in the first place.

Once he knew Sophia was safe home, he sent her a miniature portrait of her he had painted from memory. Doubtless she looked at it wistfully, aware she looked nothing like that now and, knowing how romantic Marc was, probably wondering if she ever had. One day he carved her initials on a tree and in drawing the S suddenly saw the solution to a problem he was having in the design of an invention he was working on. Not even for Sophia did the romantic in him distract the eye of the engineer.

His invention was for the mechanical production of the pulleys, known as blocks, that seamen relied on for hauling sails up and down. Having heard that in Britain the building of much needed warships to meet the threat from Napoleon was always held up by the absurdly long time it took to make the necessary blocks for it – they were each largely made by hand and a 74-gun ship required over 900 of them – Marc put his mind to designing a set of efficient machinery.

From General Hamilton, ADC to George Washington, he obtained a letter of introduction to the First Lord of the Admiralty in Britain, Earl Spencer. Armed with this, he set sail for England, confident that what he had to offer the Royal Navy would itself make him enough to marry and provide for Sophia.

On arriving in London in March 1799, he went straight to her house. Although they had not seen each other for six years, and she was so changed that at first he did not know her, he loved her as much as ever and she him. The banns were called almost at once and within three months they had married. Unlike most of the other engineers who generally regarded their devoted wives as the keepers of their homes and guardians of their children, Marc treated Sophia as an equal partner, shared with her his work and all his problems and often said that without her he would never have achieved anything.

To start with they had little but love to live on. The letter of introduction to Lord Spencer had so far met with no response. So through one of Sophia's brothers who worked for the Navy Board, Marc got in touch with the firm that at that time supplied the navy with its blocks and offered them his ideas. They replied that they were very happy with the way they had worked for the last twenty-five years and could see no need for a machine 'as wholly yet untried'.

By now Marc had patented his invention and in Henry Maudslay, a man as quiet as Marc was demonstrative, found a brilliant craftsman to make the working models he needed. The father of machine tools, as Maudslay would one day be dubbed, was to play a vital part in the development of all engineering of the period.

Never at any time downhearted, Marc had other ventures on hand he believed in too. He invented a duplicating machine. Aware from his own experience of the long hours spent by clerks laboriously copying drawings and documents, he was excited by the idea that, if a pen could be held in a device so its movements could be simultaneously reproduced by another on a separate sheet of paper, much time could be saved! The businessmen of London would surely see how useful he could be to them, however blind to his talents the Admiralty remained.

The government fell, and suddenly Earl Spencer was no longer First Lord. As if only then did he have time to read letters, within days he asked Brunel to see him at his London home in the village of Wimbledon. There Marc must have displayed his charm to the full, for although the business part of the meeting did no more than send him and his patent down to Portsmouth to be examined by the Inspector of Naval Works, socially it led to a personal friendship with the Spencers and an introduction to high society. The Earl's wife had difficulty shuffling cards for the games of patience she played owing to arthritis in her fingers. Marc promised to invent a card shuffling machine for her, which, much to her delight, he later delivered. From then on he was doubtless the talk of the salons.

In Portsmouth he learnt to his alarm that the Inspector of Naval Works who would judge his invention had himself just devised machinery for the mass-production of ships' blocks. But Sir Samuel Bentham was too big a man not to recognise that Marc's invention was more effective than his own, so he gave it the go-ahead, though, thanks to the notoriously obstructive naval bureaucracy, it was a long time before terms were agreed with Brunel. The contract went to Maudslay, but with forty different machines to make, he needed time himself. Delivered in batches to the Dockyard, they were gradually installed by Marc in a specially designed workshop and production began.

By mechanising each stage in the making of a block, it became the first ever production line, needing only 10 unskilled men to do what had formerly taken 110 craftsmen. That the hand workers employed by the firm that originally supplied blocks had now lost their livelihood – their contract with the Admiralty ceased when the Brunel machinery got going – was probably not a matter that Marc even thought about. But their plight was nothing to the social effects of his next invention, a steam-driven circular saw of such huge diameter that the cutting edge on its circumference could slice through timber and cut a 12 ft plank from it in thirty seconds. It was so precise, efficient and powerful it was sought by sawmills everywhere. At the same time Brunel invented a machine to cut wood veneers that became such an aid to cabinet-makers it dramatically reduced the price of furniture.

Only Maudslay at that time could make machinery to the minute accuracy Brunel's designs demanded, so the two men benefited from each other. Besides setting up a sawmill of his own in Battersea, Brunel now turned his experience in mass-producing blocks for the navy to devising machinery to mass-produce boots for the army. The need for this had been brought home to him at Portsmouth on seeing the state of Sir John Moore's bedraggled troops returning home from Corunna. After setting up his factory and having it visited by influential friends he'd got to know through the Spencers, he got an order to supply the army with all the boots he could produce.

So early in 1814 when his son Isambard – born in Portsmouth to become a brother to two older sisters – was about to be sent to school in Hove, it is not surprising his father believed he could well afford the fees. By now the Admiralty had at last paid him what his contract had stipulated for the use of his block-making patent – a sum equal to the amount that his machinery would save the Exchequer in the first full year of production. In the short term the government benefited because it would be a while before the overall saving could be calculated and until then they had only to pay Marc a small salary and expenses for running the workshop. But in June 1810, after constant badgering from Brunel, they had at last coughed up what was due – £17,093, a vast amount of money in those days. So Marc could afford not only to send Isambard to boarding school in Hove, but also to buy an expensive house in London, on the Thames at Chelsea, for the family.

Directly opposite, on the other side of the river, was his profitable saw mill. But one night it was burnt down, and it was discovered that although only four months earlier there had been £10,000 in the company's bank balance now there

Marc Brunel (left) *and George Stephenson* (right) *had very different personalities, but each had a son whose fame as an engineer would one day more than match his own.*

was only £800. Whether this was the result of embezzlement by some of Marc's business partners, or simply through his own financial incompetence, he was fortunate to have a bank that allowed him enough credit to get on his feet again.

And then the war ended. With Wellington's troops disbanded after Waterloo, there was no longer a need for army boots. Having been encouraged to go on producing them, Marc demanded compensation. None was forthcoming so he was forced to sell off the latest batch he had made at a heavy loss to whoever would buy them. Nevertheless, on the credit allowed him by his bank, he prospered enough with his various projects for his family to flourish.

In his holidays from school young Isambard amused his sisters with conjuring tricks he had learnt, impressed them with his ability to draw perfect circles freehand, learnt to row and swim in the Thames, and made it clear to his mother, perhaps to her unease, that he intended to be at least as successful as his father and far more famous.

Meanwhile, that other son of an engineer, Robert Stephenson, was nothing like so happy, burdened as he was by having to educate his father as well as himself.

But he was relieved of this, and only too pleased, when George apprenticed him to Nicholas Wood, an engineer who had long admired the intuitive skill of George Stephenson and soon saw in Robert a similar aptitude, in his case augmented by the theoretical knowledge he had gained at school. But probably he also saw in him his restlessness in wanting to get away from his father's demands on him.

By now George was leading the field in the manufacture of locomotives, as well as supplying with his partner, William Losh, the strong cast-iron rails that could carry them. But he still had no reason to believe they had a future beyond the use made for them by individual collieries – till in 1818 he received a lengthy pamphlet on the future of railways, sent him by its author who was none other than the near namesake of his son, the Robert Stevenson who had built the Bell Rock lighthouse.

Since 1811 the Scottish Robert had been able to spend much more time at home. His wife continued to bear him children, though after the death of two-year-old James in 1812 she was to lose yet another in infancy four years later when she was pregnant again at thirty-seven. But inured to such tragedy by the strength of her spiritual life and the good works she did in the town, she seems to have become a fairly stern matriarch. Robert, always a man's man at heart, got on well with his boys once they were no longer babies; from London in 1816 he was writing them long chatty letters – 'Londoners are not so tall or strong as Scots because instead of porridge they eat cakes!' – and in a letter to Jeannie he begs her to try to go out more and be more sociable while also daring to ask why the boys are not allowed to eat strawberries if they so like them.

The Bell Rock lighthouse had made his name. He was consulted on the deepening of rivers, enlargement of quarries, improvements to harbours, repairs to bridges, and for the town of Arbroath how best to preserve the crumbling ruins of the ancient Abbey. He added an office to the family house at Baxters Place where he wrote his reports and surveys. He was acquiring as much prestige in Scotland as John Rennie had ever had.

And he had become fascinated by the possibilities inherent in horse-drawn railways. Long before they were being seriously considered in England for the conveyance of passengers, he was checking out for interested parties possible rail routes between Perth and Aberdeen, Glasgow and Edinburgh, Edinburgh and Berwick. In November 1818 his plans for a line from Brechin to Montrose were adopted; and in making recommendations for a railway from the coalfields of Midlothian to Edinburgh and Leith, he wrote for its sponsor a *Report on*

Railways that confimed his position as Scotland's leading authority on the subject.

In it he pointed out that on a level railway a horse can haul over ten times as heavy a load as it can on a road, and though a horsedrawn barge can carry just as much on a canal, the capital cost of digging a canal is considerably greater than that of laying a railway. Moreover, if malleable iron as distinct from cast-iron is used for the rails, it is not likely to snap under the weight it must sustain. He singled out the work of George Stephenson in this field, crediting him with 'the most striking improvements in railway systems'. Although he had not yet met him, he corresponded with him and may well have been instrumental in bringing him to the attention of the man most responsible for creating the world's first public railway, the Quaker industrialist of Darlington, Edward Pease.

Unlike the collieries on the Tyne that employed Stephenson, those in the south Durham coalfields near Darlington had no direct access to a navigable river. So in getting their coal to the lucrative market in London they were always undercut in price by their Tyneside rivals. In 1810 a group of industrialists including Edward Pease had broadly agreed that their coalfields should somehow be linked with Stockton on the river Tees, whether by a horsedrawn railway or a canal.

In 1812 John Rennie had been consulted, and three years later he eventually delivered his report, advising a canal that he costed at £205,618. Since this kind of money could not be found, the subject was dropped. But in 1818 Pease and others became strongly in favour of a railway and asked George Overton, who had laid the tramway in south Wales that Trevithick's Penydaren locomotive had used, to survey a route. But after he'd completed it they were not very happy with it, so they asked Robert Stevenson, whose reputation as an authority on railways had spread south of the border, to check it out for them – in consultation with John Rennie.

Robert had no objection, but Rennie was indignant, perhaps even sensing that with Robert now regarded as on much the same level as himself, he might even be expected to play second fiddle to him. 'I am accustomed to think for *myself*,' he wrote testily, 'in the public works in which I have been engaged, most of them of infinitely greater magnitude and importance than the Darlington Railway. If the subscribers have not sufficient confidence in me, I decline all further concern with it.'

So it was Robert alone who checked out Overton's route, making some suggestions of his own in what he called 'a perambulatory survey'. By now he had long since met George Stephenson – in January 1819 he'd gone to Killingworth

Edward Pease, the Quaker industrialist, is often regarded as the father of railways himself for his Stockton–Darlington railway and for the faith he had in George Stephenson as engineer.

specially to talk to him – and, given his position as consultant on the proposed railway, must surely have commended him to Edward Pease as someone more qualified than Overton to survey and engineer the line. Certain it is that on the day the Act of Parliament was passed that allowed the railway to be built George Stephenson, accompanied by Nicholas Wood (to whom his son was apprenticed), arrived at Mr Pease's home.

The story once told that they simply turned up out of the blue to beg Pease to use locomotives on his railway, and that he not only agreed but took such a liking to Stephenson that he at once offered him the job of engineer, has long been discredited. The fact is that, feeling let down by Overton, Pease needed someone to replace him and, whether prompted by their Scottish consultant or not, invited Stephenson to call on him.

Certainly he was impressed; he offered him the job the very next day. But Stephenson was not all that interested. In fact, he only accepted the offer on condition it did not interfere with his other work. As for locomotives, Pease agreed that night merely to have the Act of Parliament amended so it would be legal to use them if ever thought desirable.

That he needed more persuasion about locomotives probably explains a letter George wrote to Robert a few weeks later. Having noted the Scotsman's enthusiasm for malleable iron rails, he referred to some being made that in his view were far superior to the cast-iron ones he and Losh were supplying – 'they make a fine line for our engines as there are so few joints'. He went on to say that:

on a long and favourable railway I would stent my engines to travel 60 miles per day with from 40 to 60 tons of goods. They would work nearly fourfold cheaper than horses where coals are not costly. I merely make these observations as I know you have been at more trouble than any man I know of in searching into the utility of railways.

He evidently thought that as the nationally known engineer that Robert had now become he had influence not only on the Stockton–Darlington project but on railway building generally.

Nevertheless, it was for a largely horsedrawn railway that in October that year George and his son, specially released from his apprenticeship to Wood, set off together to make a detailed survey of the line from Darlington to Stockton. Little did George know that before the railway was built he would no longer have his son at his side. But at that time Robert didn't know that either.

CHAPTER EIGHT

Dreams across the Ocean

In May 1821, when the Act of Parliament was passed to let the Darlington–
Stockton railway go ahead, young Isambard Brunel – at fifteen just three years
younger than Robert Stephenson – was at school in Paris. He had been sent there
by his father to be coached at the Lycée Henri IV for entry into the science and
engineering university, the Ecole Polytechnique. It was there he heard that in
London his father had been thrown into the Kings Bench prison for debt.

Sophia had insisted on accompanying her husband. A debtors' prison was a
luxury hotel compared with where she'd been incarcerated during the French
Revolution. And Marc, not known ever to have cared very much about his
creature comforts, simply got on with his work.

Long before his arrest he had been asked by the Czar of Russia to design a
bridge over the river Neva. Ice floes ruled out masonry piers so he had proposed a
gigantic arch from bank to bank made of bonded wood, or perhaps a tunnel which
he would be happy to engineer for them. Many years ago his insatiable curiosity
had led him to ponder how the ship-worm which did such damage to timbers
managed to burrow without being engulfed by the dust it created. On discovering
it had a kind of cowl over its head, an idea came to him for a tunnelling machine
that could be similarly protected. He had already patented it and, despite his
surroundings, was now busily working on it.

It was probably his two daughters who most felt the shame of what had
happened to their father. The eldest was now married and the next one, Emma,
was doubtless hoping to be soon. Yet all their efforts to get their father released
were in vain; so were those of Earl Spencer to whom Marc had written at once for
help.

It was the failure of Marc's bank that had brought on what the family ever after
referred to as 'the misfortune'. Once it was known his cheques would no longer be
honoured, his creditors closed in at once. Although the government now owed him
nothing, Marc maintained that if they wanted him to work for them in the future, as

he had done so magnificently in the past, it was up to them to make that possible. He let it be known that the Russians appreciated his services even if the British didn't, and would surely pay his debts if he agreed to go and work for them.

His blackmail did the trick. It took several months but after questions had been asked in Parliament, notably by the Duke of Wellington no less, he received £5,000 on condition he stayed in Britain. It was enough to get the family back into their Chelsea home, but it left them almost nothing to live on.

So when Isambard failed to make the grade for the Ecole Polytechnique, his father's disappointment was tinged with some relief that at least he'd be shot of education fees from now on. And when the boy came home, he was pleased to see that he had not just acquired a theoretical knowledge at least as good as his own, but having also learnt the workshop side of engineering from Louis Breguet, a master as much admired in France for his perfectionism as Henry Maudslay was in London, had also acquired all the manual skills of an expert craftsman.

He worked busily in his father's office. Marc had no difficulty attracting jobs again, thanks to his determination, charm and talent. He designed a sawmill for use in the West Indies, two suspension bridges to be built for the French on their Ile de Bourbon colony, a swing bridge for Liverpool Docks, and a canal in Cornwall. In almost every form of construction Isambard was able to learn so much from him.

It was a happy time for them both. Marc had long ago spotted a talent in his son that he recognised to be as great at least as his own, and for this reason could not really imagine the boy doing anything else but nurturing it. That he enjoyed swimming and rowing on the Thames, and pleasant social evenings with his married sister and her husband Benjamin was not, of course, disapproved of by his father. He just thought such frivolous pleasures were rather a waste of the boy's time.

Only his wife Sophia appreciated that by now her son may well have had an interest in the opposite sex comparable to her own at his age, and that her husband had apparently forgotten how absurdly passionate and romantic he himself had been at one time. So it would have come as something of a shock to her if she had peeped into Isambard's diary and learnt that, though at seventeen he admitted he had fallen in love, he had nevertheless decided to have no more to do with the girl because in his view she could not help with his career.

George Stephenson's son Robert was nothing like so single-minded in his ambition. He had at least as much talent as a potential engineer, but at twenty may well have suspected it was largely being used to advance the interests of his father. So once the survey of the Stockton–Darlington line was completed, he was thrilled to get a job with a man who had nothing to do with his father at all.

This was William James, a wealthy Warwickshire colliery owner whose enthusiasm for railways had led him into promoting them himself. He had already surveyed a line to carry coal from the Midlands to London, and having heard of the resentment in Lancashire about the high prices charged for use of the canal between Liverpool and Manchester, he suggested they follow the lead set by Pease in Darlington and build their own railway. This was quickly taken up by a merchant called Joseph Sandars who commissioned James to undertake a survey. Having got to know the Stephensons well by then, James asked Robert to help him with it.

They had their problems. The canal company whipped up such local opposition that they were set upon wherever they went. Farmers came out with shotguns; stones were thrown at them ; their man with the measuring chain was speared in the back with a pitchfork. Only when trying to survey the great bog of Chat Moss were they safe from their pursuers, and there one day William James fell in, sinking fast into the ooze till Robert and the others managed just in time to haul him out.

In sharing these vicissitudes with James, Robert developed a close affinity with the older man very different from the relationship he had with his father. With James he was under no pressure all the time to succeed, no constant admonishment; with James he could relax and simply be himself for a change. So he was really sorry when the survey was at last completed and they had to part.

Perhaps a bit jealous of this friendship, the possessive George at once despatched him to Edinburgh University. Robert didn't really know what for, but he had many friends his own age – soon to include a young man called Joseph Locke that George took on as an apprentice – and in his letters from Edinburgh he reveals himself now as a very mature and independent-minded young man.

Six months later George ordered him home to become Managing Director of a locomotive factory he was setting up. He not only intended to run locomotives on the Stockton–Darlington line – whose first rails had already been laid to the accompaniment of huge local celebrations – but also on William James's Liverpool–Manchester if it ever got built, and on other railways too now being talked about.

That Robert was wholly capable even at nineteen of running a big manufacturing concern was evidenced by the fact that his older fellow directors had no objection at all. It was Robert himself who had misgivings. He guessed his father only put him in charge to make sure he had control of it himself, which he would not have found so easy with any other MD. That George could have run the company quite openly and chose not to, even naming the firm Robert Stephenson & Co, suggests he was already unsure of his son's loyalty and trying to bribe him. But Robert could see through that. Almost any good offer from another quarter now would be enough for him to make a break for it.

It was to come from an unexpected direction. It was now ten years since Richard Trevithick had despatched his engines to Peru to open up drowned-out silver mines. When he followed them in 1816, he arrived at Lima to a tremendous reception. He was Don Ricardo, the great engineer who was going to enrich the whole country through the use of his wonderful machines. They gave him a horse and, in appreciation of the honour he had done them, had it shod with silver shoes. But when after a long trek up the mountains he at last reached the mine at Cerro de Pasco where his engines lay, everything began to go seriously wrong.

Once he'd got the engines working, his new partners found ways to ditch him. So Richard walked out and set off prospecting on his own. Discovering an untapped seam of copper, he recruited local labour and began excavation. But just as it looked like being profitable, Simón Bolívar's rebel troops swept in and all the miners fled. Returning to the now neglected mine at Cerro de Pasco, he had just re-established his authority there and got everything in full working order when the rebels took possession of this district too. They destroyed the mine as a symbol of the riches enjoyed by their hated Spanish masters and in front of Trevithick's eyes systematically smashed to smithereens each of his steam-engines.

All this time he had sent no word home whatever and by 1824 it had long been assumed he was dead. Yet despite the misfortunes thought to have befallen him, the dream of untold riches to be had from ancient flooded silver mines in South America was still tempting others to follow him – such as Robert Stephenson.

It was his father that the Colombian Mining Association approached first. His knowledge of mining generally, and of the kind of machinery needed to pump out the water of centuries and give access to the lucrative veins of silver and gold still waiting to be tapped in Colombia, was what they sought first. But after dangling the bait that, if their excavations prospered, a big market for Stephenson engines would open up out there, they asked if his son could be released to come and help them. They'd have tried to get George himself, they said, had he not been so heavily engaged on the Stockton–Darlington railway, now nearing completion, and on his other railway ventures too.

Edward Pease and the other directors of the newly formed locomotive company were none too happy, and George most certainly was not. But Robert implored him: he would only be required for a year to get the mining operation going and should not be expected to turn down such a splendid 'entry into business'.

By now Robert must have known he had become at least as good an engineer as his father, and with the same belief in the future of railways must also have known that, as the managing director of the first major locomotive factory to be set up, he was on the verge of an 'entry into business' that would take him to the pinnacles of success. Yet he was prepared to turn that down merely for the chance to make money in a land far away he knew nothing about. If any proof were needed of how strong was the urge to get away from his domineering father, this was surely it.

Told it was only for a year, George and the partners reluctantly agreed to his release. But in fact Robert had signed not for one year but *three*, though he wasn't telling anyone that. Having made the break, he went to London in May 1824, having business there anyway, and it was from there he expected to leave for America. But presently he learnt that his ship was to sail from Liverpool, so back north he had to go. And in Liverpool he met up again with his father.

Four years earlier George had remarried. Once Robert was no longer a child to be looked after, George's sister who had brought him up had left to get married herself. So George looked around for the woman he had proposed to twenty years ago when he was nineteen. As promised, Elizabeth Hindmarsh had kept herself for him, and now that he was so evidently a man of substance her father had no objection at all. But though Elizabeth was so happy to marry him at last, George does not seem to have paid her much attention. They lived now in Newcastle, close to the new locomotive works, but he had so many commitments he was rarely at home. And since Elizabeth was not Robert's mother, and indeed barely knew him, he could not share with her the desolation he felt at his son's departure.

He put a brave face on it, telling a friend that at the dinner he had with him in Liverpool a few days before he sailed 'the poor fellow is in good spirits so I must make the best of it.'

Their host that night had been Joseph Sandars, the merchant who had commissioned William James to survey the railway from Manchester to Liverpool that Robert had helped with. Since then a company had been formed, but in view of the protests aroused by the survey James had been asked to revise it. Unfortunately, his many other commitments, like a railway he had also surveyed between Canterbury and Whitstable, plus illness and major financial problems as a result of being so overstretched, prevented him from delivering the new survey by the date it was required. So Sandars had asked George Stephenson to take on the job, and James was fired.

Robert, being so close to James, was terribly upset, especially when he learnt his father had also managed to replace James on the Canterbury–Whitstable railway. His reaction had nothing to do with his decision to go to Colombia, but it certainly removed any guilt he might otherwise have felt. George confessed afterwards to his sadness on seeing his son sail away down the Mersey, but in his diary that night Robert wrote only of how he would pass the time on the voyage and made no reference at all to the father he had left behind.

And it wasn't too long before the remaining directors of Robert Stephenson & Co discovered that the man in whose name the company had been formed had not just gone on a sabbatical. That he had signed a contract to keep him in Colombia for three whole years prompted a furious letter to him insisting he come back at once. Robert is not known even to have answered it. And how his father felt when he discovered it is not known either.

In contrast, his contemporary, Isambard Brunel, had been working very happily with his father. Admittedly, his ambitions were such that he confessed in his diary how miserable he'd be if they did not come off; he had gloomy forebodings he might end up with nothing but an obscure house in the suburbs. As short in height as his father, but with a personality that would one day have him nicknamed 'the little giant', he longed to be involved with something so big it would be talked about by everyone. A *château d'Espagne* he called it, meaning a dream, a castle in the air!

He may well have thought that chance had come when his father was asked to do what Richard Trevithick had failed to do – drive a tunnel under the Thames that would be the first of its kind to be bored beneath a great river anywhere.

If there had been a need for a tunnel back in 1808 when Richard Trevithick had begun his, it was far more urgent now. Although the end of the Napoleonic wars had surprisingly led to a recession, the expansion of London docks and improvement in road and canal communications across the country gave a fillip to overseas trade that could now take place unimpeded by war and brought so many ships to the port of London that the scene on the river downstream from the City was a veritable forest of masts. To get from one side to the other meant either paying the toll to use London Bridge, a circuitous enough route anyway, or being rowed across by one of the 350 watermen who between them made 4,000 such trips every day.

With pressure now to build docks on the south side too – besides a new one near the Tower, St Katharine's, to be designed by Thomas Telford – there had either to be a bridge high enough to clear the shipping or the cheaper and seemingly more practicable alternative of a tunnel. When it was known that Marc Brunel had patented a tunnelling machine he'd not yet found a use for, he was approached by a former director of the company that had once engaged Trevithick.

Marc was thrilled by the challenge. A new company was formed and the capital raised. Marc was to get £1,000 a year as engineer, £5,000 up front to build his machine and prepare the ground, and another £5,000 on completion of the work. Neither he nor the company expected it to take more than three years at most. If he started his bore at Rotherhithe, but a little further upstream from Trevithick's where the river was narrower, he was told he'd find safe blue clay all the way and no quicksands, provided he did not make the level too deep. Events were to show this could not have been more wrong.

While Maudslay was engaged to make the tunnelling machine, Marc put his mind to digging the shaft that was required before boring could begin. How to do this without the sides falling in had always been a problem with such shafts: but not to Brunel. Simply erect a circular tower as wide as you want the shaft to be; bind it with iron rings to make sure it is always absolutely upright and rigid; put a lot of labourers inside to dig out the earth from underneath it, and it will gradually sink under its own weight. Marc had no doubt at all it would work. Thanks to him it is a technique that has been used ever since.

Although Thomas Telford twenty-five years earlier had expressed no doubt at all that he could build an iron aqueduct 120 ft in the air at Pont Cysyllte, and Robert Stevenson had been equally sure he could put up a lighthouse on a submerged rock eleven miles out to sea, they never showed their confidence as rashly and as ostentatiously as Marc Brunel did with his tunnel. Wholly undeterred by the failure of Trevithick's, without demonstrable evidence even that the sinking of his shaft would work, he laid on an opening ceremony at Rotherhithe guaranteed to bring maximum publicity.

As bells pealed from the parish church, the high society friends he had invited either stepped ashore at the company wharf from boats he had hired or rolled up in their carriages along streets festooned with Union Jacks. They were greeted by a brass band and the company Chairman making a fulsome speech about 'this great national undertaking'. With a silver trowel Marc laid the first brick of the tower that would become the shaft, before his son with equal precision laid the second. After partaking of what *The Times* referred to as a 'sumptuous collation', toasts were drunk over a model of the intended tunnel carved in icing sugar. Bottles of the same wine were then put aside to be drunk at a similar gathering to be held the other side of the river when the tunnel was finished. Little did anyone there guess how long that was, in fact, going to be.

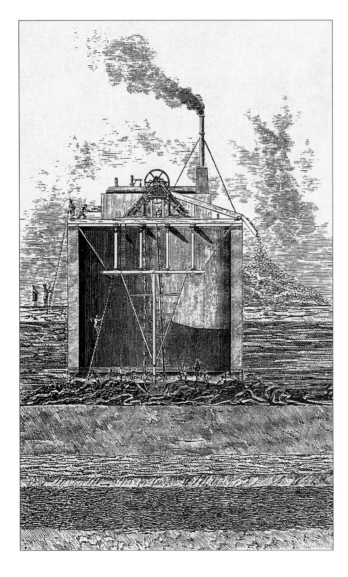

Digging out the ground beneath the shaft, so it will slowly sink under its own weight.

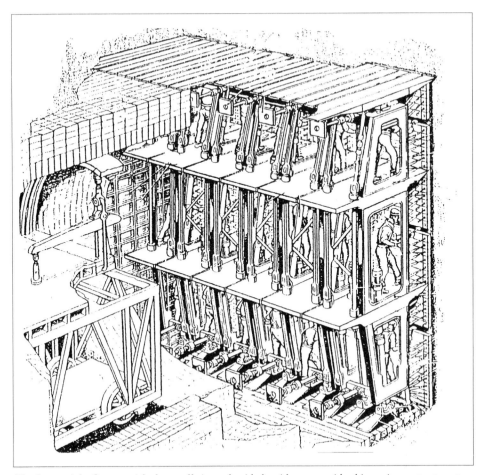

Twelve upright frames with three cells in each, side by side, to provide thirty-six compartments. In each a miner would first remove a horizontal board in front of him, dig out 4½ inches of earth, replace the board in its new position, and continue doing the same with the others till the entire frame could advance into the gap. Behind him, on wooden staging, brick layers erected arches to create two parallel passageways, seen below on the approach to them and in cross-section.

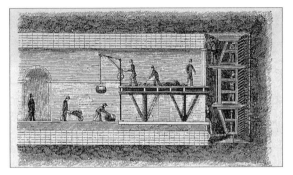

If Isambard assumed that, with his father now nearing his late fifties and not in the best of health, it would be himself in charge when the tunnel was completed, and in reaping the glory of that find himself the much sought after engineer he intended to be, his ambition was soon jolted. His father put an engineer called Armstrong in charge for whom Isambard was to work as assistant.

Nevertheless, with Armstrong he supervised the building of the 50 ft wide tower and ordered each of the bricklayers to lay 1,000 bricks a day. It took three weeks, and when completed weighed 910 tons. Now the work of digging out inside it began, a chain of buckets descending and ascending to take away the excavated soil. Slowly but surely the tower was sinking – 6 inches a day – until at last it had been lowered to the depth required. Go to Rotherhithe today and, just behind the tube station, you can clearly see where the circular shaft used to be.

A reservoir was added to drain off water that might gather in the workings, and a pump installed to get it there. A drainage channel to be dug along the line of the tunnel as work progressed had been ruled out by the directors as an unnecessary expense.

It was now time for the great tunnelling machine, whose invention had inspired the whole enterprise and on which its success was utterly to depend, to be installed. It consisted of what Marc was to refer to as the frames – twelve iron structures, each 22 ft high but only 3 ft wide, to stand side by side like books on a shelf. Together they would make up a total width of 36 ft which, unlike Trevithick's bore only a tenth as wide, was to be the general breadth of the tunnel.

Each frame had three levels, one above the other, so that when all twelve stood side by side there were thirty-six separate compartments. In each there was room for a miner, faced by horizontal wooden boards that lay across his section of the work to be excavated. His job was to remove one board, dig out the clay behind it to a depth of just 4½ inches (the width of a brick), replace the board in its new position, then remove the one beneath it to go on excavating the same way. Once this had been done by each of the three miners, their frame could be pushed forward into the gap. Above the entire apparatus was an immensely strong iron roof – the wood-boring shipworm's cowl – that acted as a shield against the weight of the ground above. Since this was so critically important, Marc often referred to his machine as simply the shield.

Once the frames had moved forward, the 4½ inch excavation was now revealed immediately behind it to be filled in at once by bricklayers. Although today the manual labour of miners has long been mechanised, as a tunnelling method the principle established by Marc Brunel in the 1820s has governed all tunnelling since.

By September 1825 each of the twelve huge frames made by Maudslay in his workshop was ready to be brought to the site. But before they could be lowered down the shaft for assembly and the work begin, an event took place elsewhere in the country that not even the nineteen-year-old Isambard, ambitious as he was and destined to become an engineer of world fame, could at that time fully appreciate.

It was the opening of the Stockton–Darlington railway.

Telford's bridge over the Menai Straits looks very much the same today, though the iron suspension rods (which had to be strengthened even in Telford's time) have now been replaced by steel ones.

CHAPTER NINE

Defeat and Disaster

Four years earlier, in 1821, John Rennie had died. He was only sixty, though the lofty condescension displayed in his writings gives the impression he was that age most of his career. It would be wrong to suggest his death marked the end of an era. His sons had much the same august manner and carried on the same tradition. Through them the huge engineering firm he had created, which included making engines and machinery as well as designing bridges, docks and canals, expanded even further into shipbuilding and marine engines. It was his second son who completed his London Bridge, which he had been working on when he died, and who received the knighthood that his father is said to have *declined*, believe it or not, when at the opening of his Waterloo Bridge it had been offered to him by the Prince Regent.

Meanwhile, Thomas Telford was still going strong. In fact, with Rennie's death he became busier than ever. And though Rennie had never thought steam railways would amount to very much, Telford lived long enough to see how wrong he was. But in the summer of 1825, when the Brunels had just begun to sink the shaft at Rotherhithe, Telford was in Wales to supervise the raising of the chains for his huge suspension bridge across the Menai Straits.

Striding out into the water from each bank were the arched masonry approaches that ended in two towers facing each other across the 550 ft gap between them. From the top of the mainland one the chains hung down into a barge where they were linked to ropes from over the top of the facing tower. To wind them in on the Anglesey shore, and thus haul them up into the air, was a windlass driven not by steam but by the muscle power of 150 men pushing it round.

As at Pont Cysyllte, thousands came to watch. It took 1½ hours for the chains to be raised till the centre of their huge dipping curve was 100 ft above the water where the roadway would hang. That it was now possible to cross the strait without going on the sea was demonstrated that very day by two workmen so excited (or so crazy?) that they crawled along the chain from one pier to the other.

Six months later the bridge was open to traffic and it was possible at last to travel overland direct from London to Holyhead. The coach trade was delighted. Everywhere the roads were being improved and, although by now the Stockton–Darlington railway had already opened, it did not seem to present in the eyes of most people any serious challenge to the supremacy of roads and canals.

The opening of this railway had, of course, caused a sensation. Huntsmen riding beside the train were amazed that not even their horses could keep up with it. Nor could a passing stagecoach, despite the fact that though the coach was carrying only sixteen passengers the faster steam train had over 600 on board.

Small though the engine was, it was pulling twelve wagons full of coal, a carriage specially built for the directors and their guests, and fourteen more for the men who'd built the line and locomotive on which dozens of freeloading passengers had added their weight as well. It was a load almost ten times as great as that carried by Trevithick at Penydaren over twenty years earlier. Allowing for the exaggeration of a sensationalist press, its arrival at Stockton was greeted by 40,000 people. To celebrate the triumph, a magnificent banquet was held in Stockton that night, the final toast rightly accorded to its engineer, George Stephenson.

Nevertheless, it has to be recognised that not even Stephenson wanted locomotive transport the whole way. For a third of the route, from the coalfields for which it was designed to just before Darlington, the traction came either from horses or from the haulage power of stationary engines. And for the proposed railway between Liverpool and Manchester, where the object was simply to break the monopoly held by the canal company, the only advantage to be gained from using locomotives rather than horses was that they might in the long run prove cheaper.

George wanted to prove that they would be. But in September 1825, in spite of his triumph with the Stockton–Darlington line, he was in no position to prove anything. If the Liverpool–Manchester railway was to go ahead at all, after the two surveys that had now been done for it, it looked like happening without Stephenson.

Earlier that year the company had sent him to London to justify the line before Parliament with a view to obtaining the necessary Act to let it go ahead. Imagine the scene: the working class Geordie who could barely read or write against the very people he most despised for the way, he believed, that their superior education made them despise him. Overawed by his surroundings, he was either

Steam road carriages could have had a big commercial future if the turnpike trusts had not charged them punitive tolls to please the coaching interests, so both were seen off by the railways.

hopelessly vague or so testy and defensive he came over as arrogant, ignorant, and incompetent. And since the opposition to the railway came from powerful canal companies and coach trade interests who together with wealthy landowners could afford the most skilful counsel that money could buy, it's not surprising that George was made a fool of and the Bill thrown out.

Looking back on it now, we tend to regard the railway enthusiasts as heroes and their opponents as pathetic reactionaries. But at the end of the twentieth century one can argue that if the railways had never been allowed to take hold the way they did the world today might not have been all that different. Telford and Rennie were not against steam locomotion as such. They could happily visualise it replacing horsedrawn coaches on roads, and in the 1820s it might well have done. Trevithick's steam carriage of twenty-five years earlier had had its successors, and several were now being built. But the turnpike trusts who owned the roads wanted to keep in with their principal customers, the horsedrawn coach trade, and charged such punitive tolls for steam carriages – often almost *twelve* times what they charged the horse coaches – that potential promoters had no incentive to invest in them at all. But if they had, one can easily imagine steam carriages operating on roads in the Victorian age with freight going as usual by canal – albeit on steamboats, a mode of transport Telford himself had checked out and found far more cost effective than railways. Many more better roads would have followed from his and Macadam's work and by the time the petrol-driven car arrived the country would have been ready to receive it. This is the kind of future Telford dreamed of.

It was also one which, at the end of 1825, could well have looked to George Stephenson as most likely to come into being. The road and canal lobby had not just seen off the Liverpool–Manchester railway but their triumph had lessened the enthusiasm of promoters for other railways too. And with no one in public life to speak up for railways generally, George had no reason to believe his career and achievements as an engineer mattered much to anyone.

Christmas 1825 would have been a gloomy time for him. Alone with his wife in their smart home at Greenfield Street, Newcastle, he must have been wondering if his son would ever return, at the same time knowing that, whatever the future of the Liverpool–Manchester railway, for the mess he made of it at Westminster he himself had now been fired as engineer.

Isambard Brunel must have known about the opening of the Stockton–Darlington railway, and being in London would have heard from many sources about the grilling of George Stephenson at Westminster that led to the rejection of the Liverpool–Manchester Bill. Yet at no point in his diary at this time does he see railway building as a field for himself; he is more jealous of the Rennie brothers than of the Stephensons. And if not even he included among his 'castles in the air' the dream of becoming a great railway engineer, that in itself shows how doubtful at that time the prospect for railways was broadly considered to be.

It was as the creator of great works in the field of civil engineering that he fancied himself, such as a canal then being mooted through the isthmus of Panama, or this grand tunnel he was building with his father. Unfortunately, at the start of 1826, this was not going at all the way it was intended to.

There had been major logistical problems. It was to have two parallel carriageways, accessible to each other through arches in a wall of masonry to be built between them. This wall running through the centre of the workings would take the weight from above and distribute it laterally in an arched roof over each carriageway. So although the shielded frames were excavating a rectangular area half as wide again as it was tall, behind them brick arches were being built to give the effect of two separate but parallel tunnels. To make production efficient, the time taken by the miners to carry out their task before the frames had to move should equal that taken by the bricklayers to do the job behind them. This took a lot of organisation. Add the presence of carpenters erecting timber staging for the bricklayers, and labourers to carry away the spoil, all on top of each other in a confined space, plus the miners not yet being skilled enough to handle carefully what the frames required of them, and their nervousness on removing their boards, and it's not surprising that work so far had been very slow indeed.

It was further slowed by the special caution needed when it was found that the firm blue clay expected was more and more being interrupted by slushy gravel and often quicksands. Since boring began at the end of November less than 50 ft had been excavated two months later. And though they were not yet under the river, water was already seeping in. Because the tunnel went downhill, it gathered in just the area where the men were working, and very foul water it was too.

In those days the Thames below London Bridge carried off all the city's sewage. The miners' trowels were full of it; its stench polluted the air that in that confined space underground was all that there was to breathe. The effect was to bring on what soon became known as tunnel fever, congested lungs, headaches, vomiting, dizziness, even temporary blindness. This was something Marc had never anticipated, and it turned out he was one of the first to suffer. He had attacks of pleurisy which soon became so bad he had no choice but to take to his bed.

To save money (perhaps even to make it) Brunel had put his Chelsea house up for sale and taken a lease on a far less expensive one in Bridge Street, Blackfriars, into which he also moved his city office. For Sophia it was at least more salubrious than Rotherhithe where poor Jane Trevithick had had to live, but it was not like Chelsea. Nevertheless, perhaps anticipating with her usual shrewdness that they might be here a good deal longer than her ever optimistic husband anticipated, she set about making a very comfortable home. Isambard, meanwhile, had taken lodgings in Rotherhithe and when, just a few weeks after his father was taken ill, the tunnel sickness hit Armstrong too, forcing him to retire (never, in fact, to return), Isambard aged twenty was left in sole charge.

It was just the challenge he wanted. A born commander, he paraded his men at the start of each shift, weeded out the drunks, docked the pay of anyone he thought had not been working hard enough, sacked those who threatened to strike, knowing how easily they could be replaced, taught them precisely how to use their equipment, and because he was seen to work himself in the stinking atmosphere of the tunnel even longer hours than they did, was not just respected as boss but loved.

One reason progress was so slow was having to move the frames every 4½ inches of excavation. If they could stay put till *nine* inches were dug out, much time would be saved. Worried that in six months the work had not advanced more than 100 ft, the directors made Marc, on his sickbed at home, agree to this. It made the miners and bricklayers twice as anxious, since twice as much ground was left unsupported before bricking in could be done, but it speeded up work. By August the bore had advanced a further 100 ft and was now under the river bed itself.

Water kept seeping in, especially under the weight of a high tide. The pumps were constantly at work. To replace the candles that had hitherto provided the only light, gas lamps were now installed. Some of the labourers were not too happy about that. Apparently they had the idea it was safer to work in darkness, since if there was no light the water would not be able to find them if it did break in.

Isambard lived largely on the job. Sometimes he spent as long as thirty-six hours at a time in the tunnel, which made his parents so worried about his health that Marc appointed assistants – Richard Beamish, an ex-Guards officer, Gravatt, the son of an artillery officer, and Riley, aged twenty-four. Soon Beamish was taken so ill with the tunnel fever he for a while lost the sight of one eye. Riley became so ill that within a few months he died. Only Isambard himself seemed to thrive. Maybe all that swimming in the Thames as a child, albeit upstream in Chelsea, had made him immune to the infection. On New Year's Eve, with Beamish, Gravatt, the foreman bricklayer and six workmen, Isambard saw in the New Year at a dinner he laid on in the workings. Three months later he gave a similar party there on his twenty-first birthday.

To keep the work going round the clock, teams were required to work in shifts which meant that altogether the company now employed over 450 men. It was such a huge drain on resources that the directors had the novel idea of admitting sightseers to come and view what was happening at an admission price of a shilling per head. To Marc's alarm the response was huge; the public turned up in droves.

By now the bore had brought them so close to the water above them that in the excavated soil the jetsam from ships was being found – an old shoe buckle, broken china, a shovel. Evidently the frames were within inches of the river bed.

So Isambard called for a diving bell. This was literally a bell whose mouth could be pressed down into the water, the air inside holding back the upward pressure from the river and allowing someone inside it, perilously perched on a crossbar from rim to rim, to breathe. A pipeline replenished the air as it was used, and in this way Isambard was able to discover that immediately above the position of the tunnelling shield there was a deep depression in the riverbed as the result of dredging for gravel. He had it filled with vast quantities of clay.

His mother had naturally been very anxious about him making this perilous descent beneath the water. But to prove to her there was nothing to worry about, Isambard invited her to come down in the thing with him herself. To Marc's alarm she excitedly agreed. Sophia Brunel was nothing if not adventurous.

Work resumed, but still the water was getting in. From now on the pumps were going all the time. Though recovered from pleurisy, it clearly wasn't good for Marc's health for him to stay long in the dank, noxious atmosphere of the workings, but his son was now virtually living there. For five days he never left the site at all, always on hand to supervise the work of each shift, and only lying down behind the frames to snatch some sleep when he thought it fairly safe to do so.

At home in Blackfriars Marc could barely sleep at all, he was so worried. At this time of spring tides he reckoned that twice a day the shield had to bear a weight of over 600 tons. Living so close to the river he'd have always known the state of the tide, as his wife would have known what he was feeling when he saw it coming in.

The sightseers kept coming in too. One day over 600 paid their shillings; the next day, over 700. Little knowing the danger they were in, they descended the shaft, walked gingerly along the bricked-up archways till in the flaring light of the gas lamps they saw ahead the massive castle of iron and its miners standing one above the other, each in his own cell, with the busy bricklayers behind them and the sweating labourers wielding their shovels. Holding their noses against the stench, none stayed long.

Until the danger from the current high tides had passed, Marc had begged the directors to keep visitors out. But they insisted they needed the revenue. Marc considered their attitude 'truly lamentable' and wrote in his diary: 'Little do others know of the anxiety and fatigue I have to undergo . . . Obliged to drive on, we run imminent risks.' But he took comfort from the strength of the shield which so far had done its job well and each day could say to his wife 'another day of danger over.'

On 15 May he came home from the workings late at night, worried that the water getting in had much increased. He found this very '*inquiétant*' as he put it and was prepared for the worst. But the next day all was well and work proceeded satisfactorily. On the 18th he went to the tunnel specially to accompany a party of fashionable ladies, friends of Captain Beamish, who wanted to view the works. He personally escorted them to the frames, and though he felt most uneasy all the time they were there, he was able to write in his diary as soon as he got home that he had 'left the works at half past five, leaving everything comparatively well'.

At the very time he was writing that, about 7 p.m., little more than an hour after he and the ladies had left, Beamish had just gone on duty and was helping the men advance one of the frames. Suddenly from somewhere came a cry of alarm, followed instantly by a crash of water bursting in with the force of a mill sluice that knocked down a bricklayer and would have swept him off the frame if Beamish hadn't caught him. As he tried in vain to reach the boards to hold back the torrent, a miner called out ''Tis no use, sir, come away, come away!'

Stumbling back, the water soon up to his waist, Beamish met Isambard and for a moment they both stared at a great wave rolling towards them which in the light of the lamps and their reflections made a spectacle, said Beamish later, 'splendid beyond description'. Boxes, timber, barrows were being swept along by it and when a small hut was smashed, the air inside it burst out with a shattering blast and blew out all the lights.

They reached the shaft where men were fighting their way up the ladder with no thought, said Beamish afterwards, 'for the situation of their comrades below'; and as he and Isambard followed, the wave from the tunnel swept up to grab at them, taking down with it in its recoil the very steps they had just climbed. They had no sooner got to the top than a cry from someone stranded was heard from below. Grabbing a rope, Isambard dropped back down the shaft to tie the rope round the struggling man and both were hauled up.

There had been 160 men in the tunnel at the time. A roll call was immediately held. Every man answered to his name.

Marc Brunel got the news from Beamish who borrowed Isambard's pony and rode along the streets of Bermondsey to cross Blackfriars Bridge to tell him. Marc took it calmly. All his fears had come true. And since nothing worse could possibly happen now, there was no more cause for anxiety. So in consequence, as he afterwards recorded, he went to bed and enjoyed at long last 'a most comfortable night'.

*

The disaster was widely reported in the press. So if Jane Trevithick in Cornwall had read all about it, her feelings can be imagined. Twenty years earlier her husband had also been driving a tunnel under the Thames, and now not even Brunel with his much vaunted machine and vast workforce had done any better. Far from it. Under a wider stretch of water her husband with a handful of men had taken his bore almost to the other side before the roof caved in. And if the company had had any gumption, they'd have backed his plan to lay cast-iron tubing on the river bed and run the tunnel through that. It would surely have worked. She wouldn't have known it, but many a tunnel even in the twentieth century has been built that way.

All Jane knew in the summer of 1827 was that the whole industrial world was now using engines of the kind her husband had pioneered; and that locomotives treated as a joke when her husband first invented them had now been running profitably for almost two years on the Stockton–Darlington railway. Even steam-driven road carriages were now being built by men who, if they ever gave a thought to their inventor, had long since stopped wondering what became of him.

She had almost stopped wondering herself. From Davies Giddy and others she heard rumours that he'd been recruited into Simón Bolívar's rebel army, that he'd been seen in Costa Rica prospecting for gold, and in Panama where he had apparently started a pearl-fishing company. The only hard news was that he had sucessfully salvaged a sunken Chilean naval ship and been paid £2,500. None of this money had ever been sent home to his wife in England, a fact that Davies Giddy could never forgive him for.

Jane was now managing an inn. It had been her brother's idea. Since he took over the family iron foundry at Hayle, he had made it one of the most successful engine works in the country. Though he could well afford to provide for his sister and her family, Jane was not one to accept charity from anyone. Since the firm owned a small hotel where its customers stayed when calling on business, it was agreed that Jane should run it. She did so with great efficiency while also bringing up her six children.

Of these, the eldest boy, who at the age of eleven had brought his sick and bankrupt father back from London all those years ago, was now in his twenties. Doubtless he remembered, and missed, his wayward but loving Dad. But his youngest brother, Francis, who was only four when Richard set him down on the quay at Penzance, after carrying him there on his shoulder to say goodbye to him before setting sail for Peru, had by now almost forgotten he had a father at all.

The young Robert Stephenson.

His contemporary rival, Isambard Brunel.

In October 1827, a big boy of fourteen in his last year at school, Francis was in class one day when a huge bronzed man in his fifties wearing a wide-brimmed hat came striding in and asked for him to be pointed out. There was a breathless silence as all eyes looked at him. To the boy's embarrassment, the outlandish stranger claimed to be his father and made him accompany him there and then to wherever he now lived with his mother. Richard's ship had docked that morning. He had come straight to the school.

His return caused a sensation in Cornwall. Receptions were given in his honour, church bells rung for him. To Jane he openly admitted he was absolutely penniless, but seemed as shamelessly cheerful and resilient as ever. He presumably told her about his adventures, all of which had proved disastrous. In Cartagena he didn't even have the money for a passage home. But as luck would have it, guess who he met there – that boy Robert, George Stephenson's son. 'Dangled him on my knee once, I told him. Can you believe it?'

They had met in a scruffy hotel, where Robert was about to take ship to New York from where he would presently sail home. Asking after his father, Richard doubtless learnt about the development of locomotives in his absence, but it seems they were uneasy in each other's company and soon parted. Robert was clearly embarrassed by the destitute state of the great Cornish engineer and, whether asked for it or not, gave him the fifty pounds he needed for his passage home.

A month after Trevithick's return Robert disembarked at Liverpool. His work for the Colombian Mining Association had not brought the disasters that overwhelmed Trevithick, but had certainly not made his fortune. He had soon longed for the expiry of his three-year contract. In letters from his friend Joseph Locke, his father's apprentice and now his most relied on assistant, and sometimes in mispelt, unpunctuated, ungrammatical missives from his father, conveying more heartfelt feeling than hard facts, he had been kept informed of events at home.

He knew all about his father's humiliation in Parliament and felt for him deeply. That it would make him more bitter than ever against the educated nobs with their posh voices and superior manners he also knew. He could well imagine his father's reaction on hearing he was to be replaced on the proposed Liverpool–Manchester railway by the Rennie brothers.

Not that the Rennies had deigned to go north themselves; they simply hired another London engineer, Charles Vignoles, to re-survey the line and try to avoid the estates whose owners had been so implacably opposed. Vignoles was not just a highly competent engineer but with his smooth educated manner, likely as that was to rub Stephenson up the wrong way, just the man to ease the passage of a new Bill through Parliament. Thanks to him, and to the hefty sums laid out to buy off the main objectors, the Bill went smoothly through to be passed in May 1827.

The Rennies and Vignoles naturally assumed they'd get the contract to engineer the line. But they reckoned without the pragmatic common sense of the Liverpool directors. Stephenson might have failed them as their advocate in Parliament, but that could not detract from his engineering skill. They were happy to give the Rennies the contract, but wanted Stephenson engaged as the man on the job.

The Rennies replied in much the same haughty manner their father would have used – that willing as they were to be associated with, say, Thomas Telford or any other respected member of the Society of Engineers, they could hardly be expected to work with George Stephenson. One can imagine them thinking – what, an ex-colliery worker who can't even speak the King's English? They were taken aback to learn that, therefore, their services were no longer required.

George was now offered the contract but on condition he worked with Vignoles himself. After all, it was Vignoles who had surveyed the line to be adopted and got the necessary Act of Parliament passed. He was entitled to be put in sole charge. When asked to work with Stephenson, he could well have taken the same lofty tone as the Rennies and walked out in disgust. But he needed the work.

He didn't have it long. Stephenson had no choice but agree to partner him, though he seems to have determined to be rid of him. He set him up as a scapegoat for mistakes that were in fact not his at all and had him dismissed. George was nothing if not ruthless when he wanted his own way. And his own way this time was to prove to those toffee-nosed snobs down south that for all his rough Northumbrian ways and lack of schooling he could build a major railway without any help from the likes of them.

It was to such a man, more determined and forceful than ever, that his son returned in November 1827. But if George thought Robert would now resume the role of dutiful son, he was in for a surprise. Robert had matured out of all recognition through his three years away, having commanded men in the most trying circumstances and met the most demanding challenges without his father being anywhere near him. Yes, he was willing enough now to take on his responsibilities as head of the locomotive company that carried his name, Robert Stephenson & Company – *his* company, not George's.

CHAPTER TEN

The Old Men Bow Out

'The Turkish power has received a severer check than it has ever suffered since Mahomet drew the sword. Just as that wine-abjuring prophet conquered by water, upon that element his successors have now been defeated. So my toast when we meet to celebrate the expulsion of the river from this tunnel is – Down with water and Mahomet! Wine and Codrington for ever!'

Raising his glass to Admiral Codrington who had just destroyed the Turkish and Egyptian fleets in the battle of Navarino, a high ranking member of the Foreign Office, and close friend of Marc Brunel, was proposing a toast at a banquet held not in Whitehall or St James's Palace, but in a 550 ft long chamber beneath the river Thames.

Immediately after the tunnel had flooded Isambard sent for the diving bell and did not merely go down in it himself to inspect the damage, but with his father's nose for good publicity, took a reporter with him – resulting in a colourful front page story in the *Standard* (its very first issue) about his determination to win through whatever the setbacks or danger. This was just what was needed to reassure the shareholders.

The hole made in the riverbed was such that Isambard found he could step from the diving bell directly onto the roof of the shield and the brickwork behind it. To fill it all kinds of suggestions were put forward by the public, including a proposal to plug it with old mattresses. In theatres like the popular Coburg across Waterloo Bridge (later to be renamed after Queen Victoria and later still as the Old Vic), audiences delighted in burlesques about the hole in the Thames as much as readers were amused by the many cartoons in the press. From ships moored in the Thames came protests which seemed to imply that unless the hole was stopped up very soon the river itself might drain away.

By now, the summer of 1827, the Brunels were plugging it with bags of clay – thousands of them (19,500 cu ft altogether), bound together with hazel sticks and tightly wedged so that they'd form in time a solid coagulated mass. Pumping could now begin, and as the water inside began to go down Isambard took a punt along the workings till it grounded on the silt that embedded the shield. From there, at the risk of his life, he crawled out to check if the clay bags were doing their job and what damage there was to the shield. His love of the spectacularly grand, made more exciting than ever by any danger attached to it, was to infuse him during most of his career, and he expressed it now in his diary:

> What a dream it now appears to me! Going down in the diving bell, examining the hole! The novelty of the thing, the excitement of the risk attending our submarine excursions, the crowds of boats to witness our works. . . . Our excursions to the frames, the low, dark, gloomy, cold arch, the heap of earth hiding the frames and rendering it quite uncertain what state they were in and what might happen, the total darkness only rendered distinct by the glimmering light of a candle or two carried by ourselves, crawling along the bank uncertain whether the ground was secure, at last reaching the frames, choked up to the middle rail.

Isambard descends in a diving bell to examine the hole in the river bed.

After the hole has been plugged Isambard takes a punt up the flooded workings and crawls over the mud to examine the state of the shield.

As the water continued to subside and no more came in, distinguished visitors were taken in punts to peer at the shield engulfed in the mud. On 18 June the Duke of Wellington celebrated the anniversary of Waterloo by coming himself to view the scene.

Nevertheless, despite the optimism in all the publicity, the Board soon had to report that out of the £179,000 invested only £25,000 remained. And the tunnel was still not even halfway across. But it had to go on, so work now resumed, though it wasn't till November that the last of the flood water was finally pumped out.

It was to celebrate that, and give new heart to the Board with the massive publicity it would attract, that the Brunels decided to hold a banquet in the tunnel for rich and influential friends. Captain Beamish called on the Colonel of his former regiment, the Coldstream Guards, and persuaded him to let the regimental band come and play. A kitchen was set up, chefs employed, waiters engaged to serve at a long table laid for fifty guests, lit by gas-lamp candelabra and under crimson draperies hanging from the arches. In the parallel tunnel another long table was set for a hundred of Brunel's most loyal workmen.

With the band of the Coldstream Guards, resplendent in their uniforms, playing patriotic marches that resounded to wonderful effect in the chamber of the tunnel, the guests in their finery, the long line of glittering gas-lights reflected in the table silver, the red drapes and everyone's consciousness that above them flowed the murky river Thames, made just the kind of grand dramatic scene that Isambard delighted in. After the speeches, he joined the workmen in the other tunnel where they presented him with a ceremonial pickaxe and spade. 'Symbols of the miner's craft' is what Beamish called them, but they were more than that. As a boss, young Isambard drove the men hard and never once took their side when they demanded more pay or better conditions. But he could work physically as hard as any of them; the tools they gave him were to show their appreciation of that.

The lack of ventilation as the job progressed brought more and more sickness. Men would go down, literally, with sudden attacks of giddiness; Marc could hardly breathe down there; even Beamish was off sick for weeks with pleurisy. Only Isambard continued to thrive, pushing everyone harder and harder. By January 1828 the tunnel had at last passed the halfway mark, measuring just over 600 ft.

On the night of 11/12 January Isambard had been working in the frames with the men since 10 p.m., pleased to notice, as he said later, 'no symptoms of insecurity'. At 6 a.m., when the morning shift took over, there was still no cause for anxiety, though the tide was now coming in fast.

In his office above ground Beamish had just come on duty, supervising the changeover of the shift. He had no sooner seen the new team down to join Isambard at the frames and returned to his desk, when he heard a shout – 'The river's in!' Running to the shaft, he saw some of the men who had just gone down desperately trying to get up again, as water surged out of the tunnel beneath them to throw up more men, among them Isambard.

As his seemingly lifeless body was swept up by the wave, Beamish just managed to grab him before he was carried back down again, hauling him to safety on the staircase. 'Ball! Collins!' cried Isambard desperately.

He said later he had just started work with the new shift, among them the two miners he most respected, Tom Ball and John Collins, when on removing a board to expose the next bit of ground to be dug out it 'swelled suddenly and a large body of water burst through. The rush was so violent the men were thrown back behind the frames. Seeing no possibility of opposing the water, I ordered all to retire.'

They needed no orders. As they stumbled back through the rapidly rising torrent – they had 200 yards to go before they reached the shaft – it built up so fast that 'the agitation of the air above it,' as Isambard described it, 'extinguished all the lights.' Wading on, they were up to their waists in the water, when some timber collapsed overhead and knocked them down:

> I struggled under water and at length extricated myself – till forced by the
> water I gained the eastern arch where I got a better footing and paused to

encourage the men who had been knocked down with me. I was anxious for Ball and Collins who I felt sure had never risen from the fall we had had and were crushed . . . But the water had risen so rapidly I was out of my depth, and my knee so injured I could scarely climb. It was the rapidly rising water that eventually carried me up the shaft where I was received by Mr Beamish.

Beamish said afterwards that 'Ball! Collins!' were the only words he could utter, and next day *The Times* reported that the men who escaped were soon seen 'carrying their fainting comrades to the public house The Spread Eagle where they were brought to by restoratives'. It went on to say:

> In a few minutes the melancholy tidings were known throughout Rotherhithe. The consternation which pervaded among the wives and children of the workmen, and their anxiety to see their husbands and parents, were most afflicting. A muster of the workmen was ordered and the following are those whose bodies are now below in the water of the tunnel. Thomas Ball, leaving a wife; John Collins, leaving a wife and two children; Thomas Evans and W. Seton, both single men; John Long, leaving a wife; Jephtha Cook, leaving six children orphans.

Isambard ordered that the diving bell should at once be lowered to find out the cause of the disaster. Too badly injured to go down in it himself, he gave directions from a barge and refused all medical attention till the bodies of the six drowned men had been recovered. Afterwards carried to his lodgings – 'I never felt so queer', he said, 'I could not bear the least shake' – he was visited by numerous doctors and, in the words of *The Times*, 'imperatively constrained to keep to his apartment where his mother, who does not ordinarily live there, has taken up residence to extend that maternal attention which the situation requires.'

It was now up to Marc, old as he was and in poor health, to take charge. He had 4,500 bags of clay wedged into the new hole and set about pumping out the water. His son, meanwhile, took a long time to get better. Besides his many visible injuries, there was clearly something wrong internally too that doctors could only guess at. Given the state of medicine at that time, whatever they prescribed probably did more harm than good. After a few weeks in Brighton where he had hoped to recuperate, he came home to his parents' house in Blackfriars so ill he had to take to his bed. For weeks he lay there bitterly reflecting that whereas the young Rennie brothers had already made their name, he himself was now merely associated with what everyone could see was a total disaster.

By midsummer his father had drained all the water from the tunnel and was ready to resume work. Only there was no more money. The Duke of Wellington launched an appeal, but it raised nowhere near enough. So the great shield was abandoned where it lay, halfway across under the Thames, and a mirror placed in front of it to reflect the glory of the splendid but useless arches that led to it.

Marc, who used to enjoy so much taking friends round the busy work-sites of his undertakings, could only bring them now to view a mere might-have-been. Lit by its gas-lamps, it made a very pretty sight for those who strolled along it for 200 yards to reach nowhere in the end but their own reflections. It was not long before Isambard wrote firmly in his diary 'The tunnel is dead!'

Seven years earlier in 1821 Thomas Telford, at the age of sixty-four, had bought his first house. Until then he had spent so much time on the move – up and down the country in bone-shaking stagecoaches and thoroughly enjoying it – that he never even thought of having a settled home.

A confirmed bachelor, who always carried needle and thread so he could darn his own socks when he had to, proud of his self-sufficiency and simple tastes, he used a coffee-house in London as his permanent address – really a small hotel at Charing Cross where the same suite of rooms was always made available to him, where his mail could be sent and where, when not away travelling from one distant location to another, he could usually be found.

In 1821, however, on the death of Rennie, he found himself so constantly sought after in London he was persuaded to live the way other men of substance did – in a proper house with servants to look after him. Moving to Abingdon Street by the Houses of Parliament on the river at Westminster, he loved showing visitors his carefully chosen furniture and the Canaletto painting he had on his wall.

His wide circle of friends all knew how welcome they'd be if he happened to be at home when they called. They ranged from influential men in government to contractors and foremen he had worked with, from the sons of Matthew Davidson, born at Pont Cysyllte during the building of the great aqueduct, to visiting foreign engineers and men of letters like the Poet Laureate, Robert Southey. Even now Telford still wrote poetry himself.

It was just as he set up house that he was invited to become President of the newly formed Institution of Civil Engineers. This had nothing to do with the snobbishly exclusive Society of Civil Engineers that the Rennies belonged to, which had been derived from their father's Smeatonian Society and was no more than a gentleman's dining club. Far from it, the new Institution was to represent all the working men of the profession whatever their social background, and if Thomas Telford were to head it it would carry enormous weight and influence. Indeed, he made such a success of it that the Rennies themselves had to join, Sir John too becoming President in 1845. Even then, though, in his inaugural address Rennie chose to belittle the work of their founder, the humble shepherd's son, and as the father of civil engineering extol instead his father's revered hero, John Smeaton.

In 1828, however, despite his acknowledged position as the Grand Old Man of the profession, Telford was still very active. His St Katharine docks begun in 1825 were now more than half finished, and canal companies, seeing the threat that might come to them from railways, were desperate for his services. They knew work was going ahead on the Liverpool–Manchester line, and broad plans already made to extend down to Birmingham. To meet this challenge a canal from Birmingham to Merseyside was needed as soon as possible and Telford agreed to engineer it.

His preference for roads and canals over railways was well known. So the directors of the Liverpool–Manchester railway were not optimistic when they applied for a government grant of £100,000, knowing that to judge such applications it was Telford that the Exchequer called on.

Insulted at having his engineering work examined by anyone, let alone by Telford, George Stephenson refused to co-operate with his inspectors. So Telford had to go up there himself and at the age of seventy-two personally walk the whole line. He was shocked by Stephenson's wasteful and inefficient methods and in his report said so. Accusing him of bias, the company publicly stuck up for their engineer but privately compelled him to be more businesslike so that they could get the grant.

When Telford eventually recommended they should have it, he added that in his view it was a false economy to avoid earthworks and then depend on fixed engines to haul loads up inclines. If there had to be gradients, it would be better to use for the entire route either horses or locomotives that could manage them. Even Stephenson at this time had never imagined using locomotives *exclusively*, but now that, thanks to Telford, this was accepted as the only alternative to horses, he was given his chance to prove once and for all that they could do the job.

It's ironic to think that, at the trials set up by the company to judge the merits of locomotives, the Stephensons' triumphant success with the *Rocket*, which finally opened up the future for steam-powered locomotives on railways all over

Convinced that Brunel's plan for the Clifton suspension bridge had too wide a span to be safe, Telford narrowed the gap in his own design by making no use at all of the cliffs and proposing two Gothic towers in their place.

the world, owed a lot to a shrewd and timely intervention from that Colossus of Roads, Thomas Telford.

At just this time Telford was pivotal in the career of another engineer too. Asked to judge the entries for a competition to build a bridge across the Avon gorge at Clifton, Bristol, he appreciated that by far the most interesting came from a young man called Isambard Kingdom Brunel. By then Telford's own suspension bridge over the Menai, the largest in the world, had proved so unstable under high winds that massive extra strengthening had had to be put in hand. So when Telford saw that Brunel's design had a span even wider, he considered it dangerous and rejected it – along with all the other entries submitted. Asked to come up with a design of his own, he happily did so. It was an extraordinary structure, standing on two Gothic towers rising from the river-bed itself. It caused great excitement.

Isambard was disgusted, as well he might be. After finally recovering from the illness brought on by the tunnel disaster, he had gone to convalesce with his mother's relatives in Plymouth, and then to other family friends at Clifton, Bristol. Here one only has to think of him walking the Clifton Downs on the edge of the great gorge, looking down at the ships far below threading their way along the river towards the Atlantic and the New World, to guess how his restless imagination was stirred. So the announcement of a competition to design a bridge for this immense ravine could not have been better timed for him. Here at last was his chance to be launched on the path to glory he aspired to. Assisted by his father, whose knowledge of suspension bridges led him to doing most of the detailed work, he submitted his design and waited for the prize.

When the judge in the competition virtually awarded it to himself, Isambard shook the dust of Bristol off his feet and headed north. Aware by now, if rather belatedly, that there might be something grand for him to be had out of railway building, he applied for the post of engineer on a proposed line from Newcastle across country to Carlisle. He was told they would certainly consider him if the man they admittedly preferred turned out not to be satisfactory.

Affronted, he later went to Manchester and stayed for a night with the family of Ellen Hulme, the girl he claimed to have loved since he was fourteen but didn't think influential enough to help him sufficiently in his career. He had lately condescended to dismiss his objections and renew his courtship, but now it was she, it seems, who turned him down. From Manchester he took the train on the now completed line to Liverpool and noted in his diary that any railway *he* designed would be a lot more comfortable.

By then he had heard that his Clifton suspension bridge might yet go ahead. Others had had the same low opinion of Telford's proposal but dared not say so to the old man. But they put it to him that, so that he wouldn't look like a judge in his own cause, maybe he would agree to having his splendid design entered in a further competition and impartially judged along with others. Telford agreed, knowing the man they asked to adjudicate was none other than the much respected Davies Giddy, who until very recently had been President of the Royal Society.

Giddy, in consultation with an engineer he called in to advise him, had some reservations at first about Isambard's design and only when the young man agreed to meet these objections was he declared the winner. There were three other entries on Giddy's short list. Telford's was not one of them.

So at the age of seventy-three the most acclaimed engineer of his day had been worsted by some 24-year-old whiz kid – he wasn't to know it was actually the young man's father, his own generation, who had done most of the work on the bridge. Not that he was one to show resentment anyway, not even if he may have suspected some favouritism towards Brunel from a man well known for the help he gave young protégés. That Isambard had been elected to the Royal Society in the last year of Giddy's presidency at an extraordinarily young age would have been regarded by Telford as pure coincidence, even if he'd known that Giddy's brother-in-law, John Guillemard, had been one of the members who proposed him. Certainly, Giddy, with his remarkable ability to spot talent as soon as he encountered it, would have been a fan of Isambard's long before he saw his design for a suspension bridge.

Before he had ever become a champion of Richard Trevithick, Giddy had been struck by the genius of Humphrey Davy and had been just as eager to promote the work of the great chemist. When Davy was made President of the Royal Society, he asked Giddy to be Treasurer. And when he became so ill he couldn't carry on, Giddy ran the Society for him and did the job so efficiently that, when Davy finally retired, he was asked to be President himself. But after a while he insisted it was wrong for the Society to have a President who was not even a scientist and in 1830, after Isambard had just been elected, he stood down.

He was now sixty-three, very happily married and, thanks to the fortune his wife had inherited (whose surname Gilbert he had now adopted instead of Giddy), was very well off. He was still an MP, though for Bodmin now, but intended to retire at the next election. He had recently acquired an absorbing new interest – gathering from a wide variety of different sources the words and music of almost lost Christmas carols, which he would later publish to the delight of the Victorians and of all succeeding generations.

He had, of course, met up with Trevithick again. Though not forgiving him for abandoning his wife and family for so long, he did his best to get him some financial reward for all that his inventions had done for the country. But though the government had paid out considerable sums to other such deserving beneficiaries, they gave nothing at all to the penniless Cornishman.

In 1827 Trevithick had returned to a country that had changed its very nature since he had left it eleven years earlier. Where there had once been quiet rural villages, there were now growing industrial towns. Tall smoking chimneys from factories and mills were becoming as much a feature of the landscape as the furnaces and forge hammers of ironworks and the slag heaps of the proliferating coal mines. Trevithick's high-pressure steam-engines had had a great deal to do with the industrial expansion, just as his pumping engines had helped to open up access to the coal and iron that industry devoured. He had helped set in motion a process that within ten years would have Britain producing more iron than the total output of the rest of the world put together, and *twice* as much coal. More than half the world's supply of cotton cloth would soon be coming from her textile mills too.

So it could be said he had played a part in changing the social scene as well. For it was now no longer the landowning aristocracy who ruled the roost. The grand houses that had so elegantly expanded the city of Edinburgh, and spread up the hillside of Clifton over Bristol, were not for lords and ladies, but for the families of merchants, ironmasters, coal magnates and mill owners. The society that once amused itself in Vauxhall Gardens, took the waters at Bath and paraded itself in its finery at country house balls, so gently but shrewdly mocked in Jane Austen's novels, was being progressively marginalised.

The monarchy had never been so unpopular. After the Napoleonic wars, when industry was hit by a recession and there was so much unemployment among its labour force, the ostentatious extravagance of the Prince Regent could have fanned the smouldering unrest of the people into the flames of a revolution. In 1819 the Duke of Wellington, in his capacity as a government minister responsible for law and order, had sent in troops to break up a radical demonstration by Manchester cotton workers which had made him more famous for the massacre of Peterloo than for his victory at Waterloo. In 1828 he had become Prime Minister, determined to quell both the growing unrest from a massively exploited working class and the demands of their middle-class bosses for a say in government.

The movement for parliamentary reform that might at least give democracy a chance led to such riots in Bristol that young Isambard found himself enrolled as a Special Constable. In that role he even made an arrest, small as he was but as tough as they come, hauling his captive off to the nearest magistrate. Whatever the effects on society of the Industrial Revolution, barely discernible though they were as yet, the engineers who had helped bring it about did not take sides.

In 1830, when the Liverpool–Manchester railway opened, Richard Trevithick seemed hardly aware of the part he had played in these vast changes. Locomotives derived from his own were being commercially manufactured by the young man he had had to borrow fifty pounds from to get home. Long after he'd lost interest in his own invented paddle steamer, the work of more persistent engineers had led to steamboats plying between Belfast, Liverpool and the Clyde, and regularly carrying mail across the Channel between Dover and Calais.

Trevithick's design for a 1,000 ft high column in cast iron to celebrate the Reform Act of 1832. Its height compared with that of St Paul's, Nelson's Column and the Pyramids.

Trevithick might even have been a passenger on one of these himself when he went to Holland in 1828 to see if his pumping engines could be used to reclaim for the Dutch the underwater land of the Zuider Zee. Later he went to Germany and France, and he was often in London, with friends in Highgate. Though he had been away from home for eleven years, he spent little enough time with his family now he was back, understandably perhaps.

Among his inventions at this time was a refrigerator and a portable domestic heater, neither of which he thought had a future. More likely to catch on, he reckoned, was a cannon that used the force of the recoil after firing to load the next shot. For the navy he had in mind an invention that could drive a ship by the jet propulsion of steam under water. He asked for the loan of a ship so he could instal it and demonstrate it to them. He got no reply.

Finally, as if to symbolise both the brilliant ingenuity and the apparent pointlessness of his entire career, he grew very excited about his project for a giant tower of cast iron he hoped to build in London – to be three times higher than St Paul's Cathedral with an equestrian statue at the top of it and a lift to run up inside it. What for? To celebrate the passing of the Reform Act of 1832, he said, as if Richard Trevithick had ever been remotely interested in politics.

A few weeks later he was doing some work for a millwright in Dartford, and staying at the local inn. He seems to have caught a chill and this time there was no devoted wife to nurse him. He was ill for a week and died alone. As he was found to have little or no money on him, he was buried in the local churchyard in the unmarked section kept for paupers. Since it's never been discovered where exactly he was laid, to this day he has no tombstone.

A few months later Thomas Telford died, to be buried with full honours in Westminster Abbey. He left more money than he ever knew he had. Among his bequests was £800 to the now impecunious Poet Laureate, Robert Southey.

In Edinburgh the builder of the Bell Rock lighthouse had handed over his business to his sons by now, but was still much consulted as the *éminence grise* of Scottish engineers. At sixty-two he was hardly an old man, but then George Stephenson was only fifty-three when Telford died and was already being regarded as a has-been. Not that George saw it that way, far from it; he would not go down without a fight. But a new generation had taken over – his son Robert who had just turned thirty, his former apprentice Joseph Locke aged twenty-nine, and the most thrusting and ambitious of all three, the 25-year-old Isambard Brunel down in Bristol.

The old men had no choice but to make way for them. They were firmly in control.

CHAPTER ELEVEN

No Stopping the Iron Horse

As a child Joseph Locke had never been the least bit interested in engineering. The youngest but one of seven children, he used to tell his sisters he hoped one day to become a Member of Parliament and ride about town on a splendid horse with a groom to wait on him. Or he would become a violinist. He had an ear for music, and when a violin was to be a prize in some village raffle he bought a ticket. He lost out, but did a deal with the winner, offering to run errands and do various chores in return for the violin. Having acquired it, he taught himself to play after a fashion and, to the pain of his sisters, insisted on performing on it.

His father despaired of him. William Locke had once worked at the same pit as George Stephenson when George was just a brakesman. They became close friends but had hardly seen each other since. By 1805 when Joseph was born, William had returned to his native Yorkshire and become manager of a colliery near Barnsley. He was well enough paid to provide handsomely for his large family.

Maybe that's why Joe showed none of the drive and determination that characterised the boyhoods of Rennie, Telford, Robert Stevenson or either of the Brunels. He had a comfortably secure life at home and could see no good reason for wanting to change it. From the age of seven he had been sent to Barnsley Grammar School which he had hated as much as any other boy for its brutal discipline, but being highly intelligent and quick to learn, with a gift for mathematics, he did well enough there.

On his leaving school at thirteen, his father got him a job in the office of a nearby colliery where he worked for a couple of years, neither bored nor particularly interested – till one day he decided he'd had enough and just walked out. So his father then persuaded a surveyor friend of his to take him on and teach him surveying. But this time Joe walked out after less than a fortnight – literally walked, covering thirty miles on foot across the moors till he got home. His father was furious, though he himself had kicked jobs just as impetuously himself enough times. Joe explained that far from teaching him surveying, all the man wanted him for was to help his wife with the housework and rock the cradle for their baby.

One day his father met up with George Stephenson again. It was a happy reunion, in the course of which George talked proudly of his son Robert, now at Edinburgh University, and heard in reply how his friend was nothing like so happy about his own son. 'Send him to me,' said George airily.

So in 1823 Joseph, now almost eighteen, was apprenticed to George Stephenson for three years, working largely at the locomotive factory in Newcastle. He received no pay, but then his father paid no premiums either, merely giving the boy enough pocket money to live on. Joe found he was curiously excited by the working of locomotives, and with his skill in mathematics probably had a better grasp of the theory behind them than his employer; he certainly had a better ability than George to express himself clearly.

Very soon he met Robert. They became such close friends that if anyone knew how restless Robert was, it would have been Joseph Locke. After Robert went to Columbia they wrote to each other regularly. From Joe's letters we realise how happy he'd become; there was no doubt now what he wanted to do in life.

George, of course, saw young Locke as a replacement for his son, and began to treat him in much the same possessive way. It would not be long before Joseph also stood up to him, but until then he was as happy to serve his master for the experience to be gained from it as George was to benefit from the young man's talent. He took him with him to complete the survey of the Liverpool–Manchester line, and later sent him off on his own to survey a new colliery railway on the Tyne. By the end of 1825, after the opening of the Stockton–Darlington, Locke was surveying many other lines for his master too, besides finalising the survey of the Canterbury–Whitstable railway which George had wrested from William James.

It was typical of George Stephenson, after the debacle of his parliamentary performance over the Liverpool–Manchester Bill, that with his back to the wall he would determine to hit out at all comers. So after his triumph with the Stockton–Darlington, every request he got to survey a railway he accepted whether he had time to take it on or not. If he could not send his son to do the work, he could now send young Locke. It meant that as railways spread across the kingdom he would be virtually in charge of them all. What he seems not to have appreciated is that he was simply giving Locke all the experience he needed to become at least as important, and as much in demand, as he ever had been himself.

In 1826 when George was back in favour and formally appointed to engineer the Liverpool–Manchester line, Locke had just completed his three-year apprenticeship. George took him on as an assistant – paying him so little that for that reason alone he risked losing him – and put him in charge of engineering that section of the line which included the crossing of the Chat Moss bog.

This huge peat morass just north of the river Irwell was where William James had nearly drowned when surveying with Robert. It was said that only a fool would think of running a railway over it; everything put on it just sank without trace. On George's instructions, Locke had his men make rafts of brushwood and heather that when joined together would form a path that simply floated on the surface. Lay on it all the rock and solid earth you could find and, however long it took, it would eventually sink to the bottom supporting a wall of solid ground above it. George didn't need to have the education of his son or former pupil to know that there's no such thing as a bottomless pit.

The work took many months. To safeguard themselves as they worked, the labourers discovered – being far more intelligent than their employers ever gave them credit for – that if they spread their weight sufficiently they would not sink. So they took to wearing something like skis, long flat boards that they fixed to the soles of their boots. Joe did the same, and when long before the job was done Stephenson sent another engineer to take over from him, how to walk about in this way was the first thing Joe had to teach him.

He had been replaced because George now needed him on the other end of the line where he had just got rid of Charles Vignoles for allegedly having messed up the tunnel to be driven through Edgehill to the docks on Merseyside. By replacing him with Locke, George had now got what he wanted – all the engineers on the job were his own dependants.

Although only twenty-one, Joe had already proved himself an expert tunneller on the Canterbury–Whitstable line. There he had bored through a hill from opposite sides and calculated it so finely that when they met in the middle no adjustment was needed at all to form a dead straight passage nearly half a mile long. With the same skill he straightened out the Edgehill tunnel and greatly impressed the Liverpool directors not only with his engineering talent but with the efficient way he organised the work force.

Did George see a threat to himself in the esteem in which his pupil was now held? Very soon he took him off the job altogether and sent him to survey another line he was responsible for, from Manchester to Stockport. Understandably, the directors protested strongly. George reminded them tartly that Locke worked for *him*, not the company.

That there could be rivalry between the now well known George Stephenson and a modest former pupil of his, not yet twenty-five, might seem absurd. But perhaps not to George, always jealously guarding his own position. Nor perhaps to the directors whose fears about George's slapdash business methods were soon to be confirmed by Thomas Telford's damning report on them. As for Locke, though pleased to know how well he was thought of by the directors, he just carried on serenely with whatever job he was given and didn't seem to question anything.

It was as if he knew his time would come and he just had to wait for it. He was supremely self-confident, not with any desire to prove himself like Robert, nor with the urge to win fame that drove Isambard Brunel; he was simply aware of his own abilities and that it would be up to him to make the most of them. In his letters to Robert he showed not only how much he enjoyed all the work his father was giving him, but that he was so much on top of it all he could afford to have a very good time socially too. He spoke of 'all the gay scenes my wildness has led me into', and added that 'whilst surveying, what do you think I did? Only fell in love! And (you may be sure) with one of the most enchanting creatures under Heaven!' It was with great regret he soon finished surveying in the area and had to move on. It was not for another six years that he was to meet the woman he would marry.

Joseph Locke.

*

Robert, though only two years older, had grown up so much in America he was ready to marry and settle down almost as soon as he returned. Just before he had left for Colombia – while waiting in London for his ship before learning it was to sail from Liverpool instead – he had met Fanny Sanderson, a London merchant's daughter. Now on his return, once he had re-established his position in the locomotive factory at Newcastle and all was going well there, he suggested to his father he should take on the completion of the Canterbury–Whitstable railway. This brought him close to London so that he could now court Fanny in earnest. They were engaged by the end of 1828 and married the following June.

It was just then that, following Telford's comments, the Liverpool directors announced a competition to help them decide once and for all whether to use locomotives or stationary engines on their railway. It was to be held on a stretch of line already constructed near Rainhill bridge, entries to be judged according to how far their performance could meet the exacting set of standards laid down. What mattered to George was not so much whether his own engine, built by Robert's factory, won as that somebody's at least should do well enough to end all thought of stationary engines being used on railways anywhere in the future.

All the same, one has to wonder what the history books would have said if the Rainhill trials had been won not by Stephenson's *Rocket*, the most famous locomotive ever built, but by an engine called the *Novelty*, designed and made in London by two engineers, Erickson and Braithwaite, who outside their profession are barely known at all today. With no railway in London on which to test the machine, it's not surprising it had teething troubles on its first ever outing. Had it not been for these minor problems, subsequently shown to be of no significance,

The Novelty *locomotive that came near to beating Stephenson's* Rocket *at the Rainhill Trials.*

the *Novelty* might well have carried the day. Much lighter than the *Rocket*, it could still pull just as big a load; it carried its own water instead of relying on a tender trailed behind it and at 28 mph went at least as fast. The public, who turned up in hundreds to watch, were full of admiration for it, and upset to learn that something had broken that could not be immediately repaired and it had to withdraw. 'It's got no guts', said Stephenson complacently.

Before the trials, having no reason at all to be sanguine about their outcome, Robert and Joseph Locke had together done a lot of research to prove the efficacy of locomotives over stationary engines and produced a report to that effect for the benefit of the Liverpool directors. After their success at Rainhill, it was now to be published for the interest of railway promoters everywhere.

It was typical of George's innate insecurity that just when he was riding so high in public esteem, with a railway about to open for the carriage of passengers between two major cities, powered by locomotives his own son was ready to supply, poised to take similar control over many other railways too if they came to fruition, he told his son and former apprentice that anything to be published on the superiority of locomotives should bear his name and his alone.

Robert was not bothered. He was happily married, living with his wife in Newcastle, managing the most important locomotive firm in the country, and known by now as the engineer of a few other small railways besides the Canterbury & Whitstable. At twenty-seven, confident of his future, he was prepared to humour his father.

Was it the fear that his educated son might reach heights he had never reached himself that made George so protective of his own reputation? If so, the lack of confidence he had in his own prestige was confirmed when it was not his son who stood up to him, but his ex-apprentice. Locke told him straight that though prepared to have his boss's name somewhere on the title page, the authorship of this important publication was to be squarely given to himself and Robert.

It was now seven years since the happy-go-lucky teenager had begun his apprenticeship, and four years since he had completed it. The fact that at twenty-five he could now defiantly stand up to his master was a reflection not just of the confidence he had in himself but of that which many others now had in him too.

For George there was more humiliation to come. Busy as he was, he did not have time to check the work of those to whom he delegated his responsibilities. Though the Liverpool–Manchester was designed to end at the docks on Merseyside, it had later been agreed to run a branch to another terminus at Lime Street. This meant a further tunnel, but because there was so much housing above it the necessary shafts could not be sunk in quite the right places. So underground there was some confusion about the direction of the bores; and it was now feared that two were so out of alignment that if continued they might even pass one other. To sort it out the company sent in a man to investigate whose judgement they trusted implicitly – Joseph Locke.

It was bad enough for George to have his work called in question at all, let alone have it judged by his former pupil. The possibility that the directors might now be thinking more highly of Locke than they did of himself did not, of course, occur to him, certainly not at the time of the railway's opening when his prestige seemed unassailable.

The opening day itself was disastrous. Guest of honour was the Duke of Wellington, Prime Minister for the last two years. Unpopular even in his own party for his implacable opposition to parliamentary reform, he was hated in the north for the Peterloo massacre eleven years earlier for which the cotton workers of Manchester had never forgiven him. Now he was to be carried in state to their city on this highly publicised steam train, and they were quietly planning their own reception for him.

It was partly to conciliate his opponents that the Duke had been persuaded to come. Unless he could soon get on terms with the reformers in his party, such as

The opening of the Liverpool–Manchester railway, with the special train for the Duke of Wellington about to set off.

William Huskisson, the MP for Liverpool, his government would surely fall. With Huskisson also to be a guest at the railway opening, here was an opportunity to effect a rapprochement that even the Duke could now see to be necessary.

The event began promisingly enough. For days there had been such an influx of people come to see it there was not a bed to be had at any hotel or lodging house. The streets were jammed with carriages, the taverns overflowing, and among the crowd souvenir-sellers did a brisk trade in mugs, glasses, handkerchiefs, even tobacco jars and snuff boxes, all crudely decorated with images of railway works and locomotives. On the meadows by the Sankey canal thousands gathered from an early hour to see the trains and their noisy engines, with their pennants of smoke billowing proudly back from their tall commanding chimneys, steam briskly across the viaduct on their way to Manchester.

There were seven of them. First came the Duke's train which had one of the two tracks all to itself. This was hauled by the *Northumbrian* driven by George Stephenson. On the other line, following in procession at regular intervals, came the rest of the trains. At Parkside, 17 miles out of Liverpool, the Duke's train was to stop while the engine took on water so his Grace could sit back in his carriage and review the parade of other trains passing by along the line beside him.

That is where it all went wrong. To get a better view, many VIPs on the Duke's train, including Huskisson, got out to stand between the tracks. These were closer together than they would be now, and the rails almost embedded in the ground like urban tramlines; so it was easy to be standing without knowing it in the path of an oncoming train. Spotting Huskisson outside, the Duke, in furthering the political cause, beckoned to him. Huskisson eagerly responded, but as the Duke opened his carriage door to admit him, the next train to pass was already approaching.

On the wrong side of the door, in his panic to get round it, Huskisson slipped and fell. He had a gammy leg which at times of stress would suddenly seize up altogether. Unable to get up, he had the wheels of the *Rocket* locomotive – with none other than Joseph Locke on the footplate – roll over his thighs.

'I have met my death,' he cried. But not, poor man, quite yet. In his agony he was lifted into the leading carriage which was immediately uncoupled from the rest of the train so that it could be driven by Stephenson in the *Northumbrian* not back to Liverpool – impossible since the engine was the wrong end of the train – but on towards Manchester. Twenty-five minutes later Stephenson had got up such steam he had been travelling at 36 mph and already reached Eccles. There they stopped, perhaps because Huskisson asked for a priest; they took him to the nearest parson in whose house he tidily dictated a slight change to his will and died that evening.

Meanwhile, the Duke and his party had been left marooned in a string of carriages that had no means of power to carry them anywhere. Only with the aid of a chain, miraculously found, could they be gingerly towed forward by one of the engines on the other line. At Eccles the *Northumbrian* again took over and, accompanied by the other trains beside it, steamed at last into Manchester many hours behind schedule – to be greeted by a crowd of Mancunians who swarmed onto the line waving banners and loudly demonstrating against the Duke. While they surged around the carriages, Stephenson used the loop-line here to get his engine to the other end of the train and start hauling it back towards Liverpool. The banquet arranged was summarily cancelled, if only to save the Duke from being lynched.

The trouble was not over yet. On the way back they met locomotives from the other trains that had detached themselves from their carriages to go and take on more water. Certainly they too could retreat back to Liverpool, but their passengers were all stranded in their carriages in Manchester surrounded by an angry mob. It took hours of shunting back and forth – what the Duke was saying at the time is sadly not on record – before all seven trains were linked together and hauled by a bevy of locomotives, through heavy rain that had now begun and in gathering darkness, none of the drivers having lights along the track or on their engines to see by, slowly but surely back to Liverpool. Otherwise the day went off without incident.

But next day, when the railway was opened to ordinary fare-paying passengers, hundreds bought tickets for the two-hour journeys between the two cities. In the first three months 71,951 passengers took the train, and in the following year nearly half a million. The coaches on the turnpike road were now virtually out of business altogether.

Wherever railways were being mooted, and plenty now were, promoters wanted Stephenson. Just to have his name on the prospectus was enough to draw investors. So when business interests in Birmingham joined with those in Liverpool to connect their two cities by rail and carry the line on to London, Stephenson saw himself in overall charge of what would be the first trunk-line across the country. Already from the Liverpool-Manchester there was a branch to Warrington (engineered by Robert) which could be continued to Birmingham; and while George took charge of this section, he made sure Robert was appointed to make the survey from Birmingham to London.

And Locke? Still employed by Stephenson, it was he, of course, that his boss sent off to do at least the northern half of the survey on the Warrington to Birmingham line. He made such a good job of it he was led to think he'd be appointed Engineer when the time came. But Stephenson protested at that, and when Locke heard that the Board had felt obliged to defer to him, he took the bold step of threatening to walk out altogether. He was only twenty-seven, but with all the railways he could see now were coming that Stephenson for all his efforts could not possibly keep to himself, he knew that with more hands-on experience of railway building than even his former master, he would never lack for a good job in the future.

The company knew that too and, anxious not to lose him, asked him to take charge of the northern half of the line that he'd surveyed, leaving the other half to Stephenson. Locke agreed, and within a year of starting had placed contracts for all the various engineering works required at prices almost exactly matching his estimates. Stephenson, meanwhile, busy as he was elsewhere and with his usual high-handed attitude to office work, had in precisely the same time not yet finalised a contract for anything.

The Board now insisted that Locke take over the whole route. Such angry scenes followed that the stress caused Locke a nervous breakdown. Eventually Stephenson left him to it, though it was not till 1835 that he formally resigned. By then he and his former pupil had not met for three years, and never would again.

In 1835 when Locke began building what had now been named The Grand Junction Railway for its linking of the three industrial cities of Manchester, Liverpool and Birmingham, Robert Stephenson was already engaged on continuing it down to London. At the same time, Isambard Brunel was about to start work on another great cross-country line to the capital, the Great Western Railway from Bristol.

Four years earlier, in June 1831, he had attended a grand party on Clifton Downs to celebrate the company's commitment to build his suspension bridge. Gun salutes were fired in the gorge down below, bands played, toasts drunk, and speeches made, one of which hailed him as a man who in years to come would be recognised wherever he went as the genius who gave Bristol its greatest ornament, its stupendous bridge and wonder of the world! Castles in the air? It looked like being the first of his grand dreams to be realised. Little did he or anyone else that day guess that he would, in fact, have died before the bridge was ever finished.

Nevertheless, he had made his name in Bristol and 18 months later was asked to engineer an expansion of the city's docks. Having lost its position as the country's second city and most important port after London, both having been ceded to Liverpool, Bristol was now fighting back. Improving the docks was one way to help restore trade; another was to follow Liverpool's example and link it by railway with the rest of the country. In January 1833 a company was formed to promote what would soon become known as the Great Western Railway. It was suggested to Isambard he put in a tender for building it. Two months later he was out surveying it.

By then the first Reform Bill had been passed and men like Brunel got the vote for the first time. The Duke of Wellington had been replaced at last, and amid growing unrest from so much unemployment a new radical movement for change was felt throughout the country. The young railway builders were expressions of it.

Yet it was just then, when it seemed all the old men were bowing out, that Marc Brunel, now sixty-five, got the break he had been waiting for for the last seven years.

CHAPTER TWELVE
Trains and Tunnel Triumphant

Marc Brunel was so absent-minded he once walked home in the rain with someone else's umbrella, not noticing till he got there that his own was still hooked over his arm. Though now in his mid-sixties and relying on a stick, he still preferred to travel by coach or public omnibus and would sometimes be so engrossed in his thoughts he would get off at the wrong place. So on 24 May 1833 Sophia would have made sure he used only a private carriage to take him that day to an appointment he had at St James's Palace – where he had been granted an audience with the King.

At sixty-eight William IV was four years older than Marc. He had come late to the throne, spent his early youth in the Navy and the rest of his life well away from the court; so on his accession he had more rapport with the real world than most of his predecessors. He hated the trappings of monarchy, delighted in deflating ceremonial occasions by making flippant remarks at solemn moments, told friends not to bother to dress up when he asked them to dinner, and to the dismay of his minders would sometimes nip out on his own to stroll around the park and shake hands with anyone who happened to recognise him.

He was just the kind of king for the new age. When Wellington's government was defeated, he happily sent for the Whigs though hoping they could get their Reform Bill passed without himself being involved. That was not to be. The Lords, of course, had thrown it out, and the only way to get it through was for him to use his royal prerogative and create the necessary number of Whig peers. That the centuries-old power of the entrenched aristocracy should be cut down to size by none other than the monarch himself made him seem a pariah to the landed gentry, but at his age he probably didn't mind too much what they thought of him.

He was far more interested in making the acquaintance of someone as far removed from politics or court society as the engineer who had built the famous tunnel under the Thames. And famous it was, white elephant or not. *The Times* had snidely christened it 'the great bore', but even though it led nowhere sightseers still flocked to visit it; there were special coach services to Rotherhithe, and in Kent and Sussex signs at crossroads pointing tourists 'to the tunnel'. Even abroad it was so well known that a lady visitor to Constantinople found it was the only thing in England her hosts wanted to know about.

Not only was Marc roughly the same age as his sovereign, but he too had spent his early youth at sea, albeit in a different navy. This in itself would have much endeared him to the Sailor King, as he was nicknamed. The fact that His Majesty could speak French fluently, and insisted on doing so, similarly endeared him to Marc. By the time he left he was encouraged to think that with the king behind the tunnel, a long hoped for government loan would surely now arrive.

At first nothing happened. But Marc's son-in-law Ben Hawes had stood for parliament and, with his brother's and Isambard's help, had been elected MP for Lambeth. With the Duke of Wellington beavering away behind the scenes too, Marc had reason to be hopeful. He designed a new and much improved tunnelling machine, and persuaded Richard Beamish to come back from his native Ireland and take over as resident engineer. So when the government grant was eventually announced and the first payment made, he was all set to go.

To extricate the old shield from where it had lain embedded for seven years, and to replace it part by part with the new one without disturbing the ground and risking another flood, was a highly complicated job. Add the time taken to build the new machine – which had 9,000 different parts – and it wasn't till another year had passed that everything was in place for work to resume.

The most reliable of the miners and bricklayers from seven years ago were re-engaged, joined by lads who were only young children when the work began. New scaffolding was erected for the bricklayers and plasterers, new pumps installed and a new railway laid to carry back the spoil. Beamish had appointed a young man called Thomas Page as his assistant and in February 1836, when the shield was finally in place, Page gave the order for work to resume. To celebrate the occasion Beamish ordered an extra pint of beer for each man.

For Sophia Brunel, it had been a difficult time. With little money coming in those days, it was hard to keep up the elegant home she had made in Blackfriars so they moved now even further down the social scale to Rotherhithe itself – to live in a small cottage near the shaft. The excuse was that Marc, frail as he now was, had to be nearer the job. With Beamish in charge, that wasn't really necessary at all.

But unlike Jane Trevithick, so lonely in Rotherhithe, at least Sophia had a wide circle of friends. Her eldest daughter and her MP husband Benjamin lived fairly close by, and during the two years of preparation before tunnel work resumed her son Isambard had been living in London too.

It had taken Isambard a mere nine months to complete his survey for the Great Western Railway. Fully trusted by the company and confirmed in his position as engineer, by the end of 1833 he had set up an office in Parliament Street, Westminster, to be close to the House for the time he knew he'd have to spend there arguing his case for the line. From his encounters with landowners when surveying he knew there'd be massive opposition; and only the previous year Robert Stephenson had been given a very rough ride before his Birmingham & London reached the statute book. Reform Bill or not, the upper classes were not giving in without a fight.

The kind of arguments both young engineers had to contend with at that time included the statement that if the brakes failed when a train was on a downward gradient it would be going so fast before it levelled out that passengers would be unable to breathe. And 'if the engine should suddenly stop, the whole train would be cracked in collision like nutshells.' Robert heard it stated in the Lords that 'no nobleman or any who have their own carriages would consent to be drawn along in a tail of waggons.' The Provost of Eton let it be known that if Brunel's GWR had a stopping place anywhere near the school the boys would be tempted to nip up to town to 'mix in all the dissipation of London life' and perhaps get back again even before their absence had been discovered.

Most of this nonsense was known to be such by those who uttered it. They indulged in such rhetoric merely to disguise their more selfish motives. Home Counties farmers did not seriously believe that the noise of passing trains would so scare their cows they would give no milk; what they did believe, quite rightly, was that they would now be open to competition for their lucrative London market from farmers as far as away as the Midlands or the Cotswolds.

The coach companies that ran dozens of coaches daily from London to Birmingham or Bristol had seen what had happened to their colleagues in Lancashire after the opening of the Liverpool & Manchester; and with the advance of these railways on the capital had good reason to fear the worst. What especially galled them was that it seemed only yesterday that Telford and Macadam had given them such good roads at last to ride on, yet all was now in jeopardy. The canal companies felt the same. Thanks to the proposed Grand Junction Railway, Telford's canal from Birmingham to Liverpool looked like being obsolete before it was even finished.

Since such vested interests could hardly be flaunted publicly, they relied on the landowners whose property the railways had to cross to put a stop to it all. But they soon discovered, as Robert did on the London–Birmingham, that a baronet like Sir Astley Cooper who had declared that if railway building 'is permitted to go on, it will in a few years destroy the *noblesse*' was only trying to up the offer for his land. Though it meant shelling out altogether not £250,000 as budgeted, but three times as much, the London–Birmingham bought off all the objectors in the end till suddenly, surprise, surprise, the House of Lords could see nothing wrong with railways, after all.

Isambard seems never to have doubted that the Bill for the GWR, thrown out by the Lords in June 1834, would be passed eventually. He had planned to terminate it in London near Vauxhall Bridge (with an eye to taking it south one day to the channel ports) but there was such an outcry in Belgravia at a railway passing by their first-floor windows on its way to the Thames that he ended it instead at Wormwood Scrubs – aiming to bring it in eventually to somewhere more central.

Having made this concession, while disarming opposition from other quarters too, he was so confident of the outcome he began surveying routes for railways that could become branches of it – from Bristol to Taunton and Exeter, from Swindon up to Cheltenham, with a further branch through Stroud, and eventually to South Wales where he had already been asked to survey a rail link between Cardiff and Merthyr Tydfil, a request from Anthony Hill of all people, the ironmaster, now in his sixties, who was once so sure there was no future in steam railways he bet £500 against Richard Trevithick's engine carrying iron on the tramway to Penydaren.

It was typical of Isambard that before his very first railway had even been authorised he not only saw it in his mind as the finest in the country, no matter what the experienced Stephensons were up to, but was already planning to extend it into a vast railway empire. By the end of 1835, after the GWR Bill had been passed, he was so sure of the great career ahead of him that, on the strength of the £2,000 a year he was now earning, he decided to get married; and bought the house he intended his wife to share with him before he had even proposed to her.

Her name was Mary Horsley, the eldest daughter in an artistic family that lived in the smart but country area of Kensington on the hillside between Kensington Palace one way and Holland House the other. Mary's father was a Doctor of Music, an organist, composer, and friend of Felix Mendelssohn who was a frequent visitor to the house. Mary's youngest sister, Sophy, was a brilliant pianist

*Nicknamed the Duchess of Kensington for her lofty manner, the beautiful Mary Horsley,
painted by her brother for the adoring Felix Mendelssohn before she married Isambard Brunel.*

who in a later age would have been allowed to follow a professional career. Her brother John was a talented portrait painter who first met Isambard in the company of William and Ben Hawes and invited him to his home. Even Mary's mother was the daughter of a musician and niece of a leading Royal Academician. Only one member of the family had no such interests or gifts – Mary herself.

But she was the most beautiful of them all and knew it. She had such a regal bearing her teasing younger sisters nicknamed her The Duchess of Kensington. Mendelssohn drooled over her, tenderly cherishing a flower she once gave him for his buttonhole. But it was the short, dark, self-confident engineer with his ambition and pent up energy she was drawn to, without giving the slightest sign to her sisters she was in any way attracted to him at all.

Isambard had wanted Ellen Hulme to be musical. He was himself, and he had a love of painting too. But though Mary had none of the accomplishments he once thought essential in a wife, which ironically he saw displayed everywhere else in the Horsley home, she had what he believed mattered most for his career – not money or influence, but a grand manner as befits the wife of a great man, a commanding bearing and spectacular beauty that would make all eyes turn. He would dress her in the finest clothes, provide her with carriages and servants, surround her with the most enviable *objets d'art*, show her off as the living proof of his success in the world.

Already he'd bought a grand house in Duke Street overlooking St James's Park. After their marriage Mary was to furnish it with all the extravagance her husband wanted and soon would be seen, with a liveried footman behind her, driving in the park in her green upholstered carriage in the morning and in her cream one in the afternoon. It was Mary who stopped Sophy from becoming a concert pianist; no way could she be seen as having a sister who had to *work* for a living.

Isambard had his office somewhere in the house but it's unlikely she visited it often or even that he wanted her to. Her place was in the salon upstairs where she entertained royally, sometimes staging elaborate amateur theatricals in which she herself would appear as some classical Greek goddess while from the adjoining music room appropriate music was improvised by the adoring Felix Mendelssohn on the organ or pianoforte. Isambard thoroughly enjoyed every minute of it. He had a penchant for theatre himself, loved nothing better than play-acting and dressing up – especially when he knew his office and drawing board were so close at hand he could escape to them at a moment's notice and frequently did.

It's been said there was no passion in their marriage. Certainly they didn't love one another in the way Marc and Sophia did; he made it clear in his diary he was really married to his work. But although that kept him away from Mary most of the time, he wrote to her tenderly, amusingly and at length. If he married her mainly for what she would do for his image, she was only too happy to act out the role for him. They were, in fact, made for each other.

In May 1836 when Isambard proposed to Mary – while strolling back with her one afternoon along the country lane from Holland House – Joseph Locke had been married for two years to a very different kind of woman. Phoebe McCreery was a forthright Lancashire lass, daughter of a Liverpool printer who fancied himself as a poet. He died in Paris from cholera while visiting there with his daughter; distraught with shock and grief she had somehow to get his body home. She had him buried in Kensal Green cemetery, London, presumably unable to get him back to Liverpool.

Locke had got to know her quite well by then, perhaps had even fallen in love with her. But until he was made Engineer to the Grand Junction Railway he was in no position financially to ask her to marry him. When he was – on a salary of £800 a year which Isambard Brunel would have sniffed at scornfully while Joe thought it 'beyond my expectations in every way' – she was happy to accept him. Sadly, little is known about her, though from Locke's letters she was evidently a forthright woman determined to push him in his career while protecting him from all who threatened it.

Soon after their marriage the worsening relations with George Stephenson over who was supposed to be in charge of engineering the Grand Junction put Joe under such stress it has been said he suffered a nervous breakdown. What exactly that meant at a time when medical science would have had only the wildest theories to explain it is anyone's guess: but it seems he found himself in a state of lassitude and acute depression that only his determined wife was able to deal with.

Though not in good health herself – even as a teenage girl she suffered from arthritis – she nursed him, soothed him, and at the right time bullied him till he emerged from his torpor more incisive, assured and energetic than ever. If Mary Brunel with her glorious detachment from her husband's career was just what Isambard wanted from her, thus freeing himself of all possible encumbrance, it was Phoebe's *involvement* in her husband's work that mattered so much to Joe. They too were made for each other.

Not much is known about Robert Stephenson's wife during the early years of their marriage. Having been whisked up to Newcastle immediately after their wedding in London, she must have been pleased to come home five years later when Robert became engineer of the London & Birmingham railway and took a house for them both on Haverstock Hill in Hampstead – so he'd be within walking distance of the operational headquarters he'd set up in a hotel he'd taken over at Swiss Cottage.

By then his father had left the north too. Immediately after the opening of the Liverpool–Manchester, George and Robert had both been involved in engineering a short railway near Leicester. There they discovered a coal seam which Robert was sure the local mine barely touched. George became so excited that with two partners he bought the necessary land, sank the shafts and became the joint owner of a very profitable colliery.

It was soon after this he proved himself so inefficient in his responsibilities on the Grand Junction railway that he lost out to Joseph Locke. Was that because he had really become more interested by now in this Leicestershire coal mine? It was not to anywhere on the Grand Junction route that he moved with his wife from Liverpool; it was to a large house he bought near Ashby-de-la-Zouch so he could supervise the work of his mine. His reputation as a railway engineer had spread across most of Europe by now, but he still resented the way snobs like the Rennie brothers looked down on him. An illiterate Geordie brought up in the pits? Sure, but look what he'd become – a colliery *owner*. That could have well have meant more to him in his innermost psyche than any of his engineering achievements.

So in July 1836 when Isambard Brunel took time off from building the Great Western Railway to marry Mary Horsley, George Stephenson was settled in Leicestershire as a prosperous coal magnate while his son was racing up and down the 110 mile route of the London–Birmingham railway, now in its third year of construction.

Robert had dreadful problems. In London, when excavating the deep cutting to take the railway down Primrose Hill through the fields and market gardens to Euston, the contractor found that once the blue clay was exposed to the air it began to swell – which meant he not only had to brick in the sides, but the ground too. In one place a bridge had been built over a canal only to be pulled down next day by the jealous canal company. At Blisworth the sides of a cutting kept falling in due to springs in the rock, and elsewhere a whole embankment, containing sulphur in the soil it had been built from, suddenly caught fire! But all this was nothing compared with what was encountered in trying to tunnel through Kilsby Hill.

Robert's plan was to sink a row of sixteen shafts from the bottom of which the headings would be made in each direction. But as soon as each shaft had gone through the rock, it encountered such quantities of quicksands that work had to be abandoned. Already alarmed by the rocketing costs, the Directors wondered if Stephenson was not, after all, quite up to the job. Angrily he told the company secretary: 'I know what to do. I shall pump all the water out till the sand is dry. Tell the directors not to be frightened; all I ask is time and fair play.'

He installed thirteen pumping engines. Together they extracted water at the rate of 1,800 gallons a minute. But even so it took *nineteen months* of continuous pumping before the substance of the hill was dry enough for tunnelling to start.

By then Joseph Locke had long since *finished* building the Grand Junction.

Of the three young railway engineers Locke is the least known, chiefly because he was so efficient that nothing too dramatic ever happened; he saw that it didn't. Tunnels meant boring into the unknown so he did his best to avoid them altogether. He would rather go round an obstacle than through it, or better still, up and over. Curiously, he had more faith in the power of locomotives than either of the Stephensons who made them, arguing that whatever extra coal was used to drive an engine up a gradient was balanced by the reduced amount used going down again; and that given the cost of track maintenance, not to mention the interest payments on the vast capital loans required to dig tunnels or make long detours, a short up and over route was financially a far better investment. In tunnelling you had no idea what you might find and anything that could not be anticipated and therefore costed in advance was anathema to him. He was as much an accountant as an engineer.

It was for that very reason he was soon to become the most sought after railway builder in Europe. He did not just say to a contractor 'here are my drawings of the bridge I need, now give me a price'; he supplied precise specifications, worked out for himself how the job should be done and at what cost so that, when the tender came in, every aspect could be discussed in detail and exact terms agreed before the contract was awarded.

On taking over the southern section of the line from Stephenson, he discovered that the cost of a viaduct over the Penk valley had been broadly agreed at £26,000. He was not surprised, on seeing how vague were Stephenson's specifications for it. He revised the design, made his own calculations of just what was needed to execute it and early one morning called on the contractor – a Cheshire man, Thomas Brassey, almost exactly his own age – at his home. Over a working breakfast Brassey soon realised that with Locke he did not have to make provision for the unforeseen expenditure that Stephenson's plans might have led him into; he was able to re-submit his tender at a price less than a quarter of the original.

Brassey was to work with Locke from then on – to become in due course the most famous contractor of the railway age, employing at the height of his career 45,000 men on different projects simultaneously. Of equal skill, if less well-known, was William Mackenzie whom Locke had first met on the tunnelling work for the Liverpool & Manchester. After awarding him a contract on the Grand Junction, Locke showed him the same respect he gave Brassey. Treating both men as no less important than himself, he pioneered that kind of equal partnership between engineer and contractor that has governed the success of all such major undertakings since.

Isambard Brunel treated no one as a partner. He regarded every contractor as just there to do his bidding. It did not matter too much how efficient they were because he supervised all the work himself and made brilliant on-the-spot judgements and decisions whenever called for. It meant, of course, that a lot of time and money was wasted while problems had to wait for him to get there and solve them. No wonder the GWR took far longer to build than anticipated, and the costs soared in consequence. But Isambard didn't mind that; the more expensive, the grander the undertaking, and the greater the glory. It was to be his creation and his alone.

From one end of the line to another, he raced about in what the navvies called his Flying Hearse – a black carriage driven by four horses and their coachman, the interior designed by Brunel as a mobile office, with desk, drawing board, carefully labelled pigeon holes for plans and papers, a place for his cigars which he virtually chain-smoked, seating for himself and his clerk, and a couch on which to grab some sleep when time allowed.

On the London–Birmingham Robert divided up the line between different contractors and organised them in much the same way as Locke on the Grand Junction. But several of his contractors let him down and he was forced, at huge extra expense, to take on their works himself. He is described by eye witnesses as leaping onto a passing coach, often without even his overcoat, to head up the line and sort out some remote problem, ever racing about like Brunel in his flying carriage.

The comparable image for Locke at this time was that of him *walking* – steadily along the line from Warrington to Birmingham. The walk took him three days, and he did it often, calmly inspecting progress and rarely needing to interfere.

Methodical, thorough and undemonstrative, he completed the job he'd taken on ahead of schedule and almost exactly within budget. Not many engineers had done that.

Certainly not Marc Brunel who in 1837 was once again encountering major difficulties with his tunnel. By far the worst problem now was the lack of ventilation. The longer the tunnel became, the more foul the air. He wrote in his diary:

> The men all complain of the excessively offensive effluvia that causes sickness, headaches and diarrhoea. Men today were being sick over the frames. I myself feel much debility after having been some time below. All complain of pain in the eyes. Dixon reported that twice in one shift he was completely deprived of sight for some time. On Sunday a bricklayer fell senseless to the floor.

Beamish was suffering again too. Having lost the sight of an eye through tunnel sickness before, he wasn't going to risk going blind altogether; and with his wife and child both sickly too, he used them as an excuse and resigned. Marc, who had had a stroke by now, was advised to stay in bed most of the time, but insisted on seeing samples of the excavated earth every two hours. It was Sophia's idea to have them hoisted up in a basket over a pulley at the bedroom window, so he could just reach out to examine them without having to go downstairs.

He had good reason to be worried. They now had a boat on the surface, floating over the line of the tunnel, from which bags of clay and other ballast were regularly pushed down into the riverbed just above where the shield was boring. But water was still getting in – till in August there was another overwhelming inundation. This time no lives were lost and, with Page now in charge, the water was effectively pumped out again. Three months later it happened again, and yet a third time three months after that. But always the water was pumped out and the work resumed.

Fire was the next hazard. An imperceptible gas would suddenly ignite into a flash of flame that shot like lightning across the workings. Page reported on one occasion that while one frame was throwing out a torrent of water, another 'was vomiting flames of fire which burned with such a roar that in less than three minutes they had melted the side of a pintpot'.

On every shift collapsed men had to be carried back through the now long tunnel to revive in the fresh air. Those who did not were sent on to nearby Guy's Hospital. Many a man died, including one of the assistant engineers; by which time Page himself had become desperately ill. Marc recorded:

Heywood died this morning, and Page is evidently sinking fast. I could not refrain from the reflection that all these brave men may in a few weeks be lingering under the influence of a slow and insidious poison . . . Today I sent Sullivan to the hospital, he being almost blind. On my return I was just in time to support poor Page who is in a very bad way. All over with him, I am persuaded. Where shall I find his successor?

Clearly it never occurred to Marc that, as the press had been saying for some time, 'the game is just not worth the candle'. The tunnel had become an obsession with him. Even at night he was woken every two hours to examine the earth samples sent up in the basket to his window. This meant he sometimes wanted to go at once to the workings to see what was happening. Absent-minded and frail as he was, he relied on his wife to dress him warmly, find his stick and a lantern, and stay up till he came home again as worried as ever. At the end of 1837 he reported bitterly in his diary that, despite all the effort and terrible sacrifices, the tunnel had been advancing at the rate of 'just the breadth of one halfpenny piece per day'.

But advance it did. In another eighteen months it reached the low water mark the other side. Page was now back at work, having miraculously recovered, and under Marc's supervision organised the building of the brick shaft that would be sunk, as at Rotherhithe fifteen years before, to receive the tunnel on the Wapping shore.

On 16 November 1841 Page was at the frames when one of the miners, having just removed the board in front of him to extract the next nine inches of earth, suddenly found that his trowel was clawing at red brick. Grabbing the sample then extracted, Page ran back with it, up the shaft and across the yard to the Brunel cottage where he excitedly presented it to Marc – a handful of brick dust from the side of the Wapping shaft.

It didn't take them long to break through to the open air. Isambard was then in town, a father by now with a three-year-old son. He brought the boy to Wapping where Marc, with typical panache, handed him to the nearest of the miners strung out along the tunnel and had him passed from hand to hand all the way back to the other side to become, as he put it triumphantly, the first human being ever to travel under a navigable waterway. That afternoon he wrote in his diary 'just returned from Wapping by *land* . . . To my dearest Sophia I owe this triumph.' On the night of the breakthrough he had written 'Sans toi, ma chère Sophie, point de tunnel'.

Four years earlier, while Isambard was heavily engaged on his Great Western Railway and Robert Stephenson on his London & Birmingham, Joseph Locke's Grand Junction had just opened. There were no speeches, no grand ceremony – just the departure of the first trains for Warrington and Liverpool from the Birmingham terminus at Curzon Street. What impressed the newspaper reporters was not the power or speed of locomotives that had caused such excitement at the Rainhill trials or at the ill-fated opening of the Liverpool–Manchester, but the ease and comfort of the journey. Passages from *The Times* include:

> The carriages are of the most elegant description. Those of the first class are superbly fitted up and equal if not superior to the great majority of private carriages. A bed is provided for those who choose to bear the extra charge – a sovereign . . .
>
> [On the opening day] at 7 o'clock precisely the bell rang and the train commenced moving. Those who witnessed the scene expressed their admiration by continued huzzas and the waving of hats and handkerchiefs. Having escaped the multitude, power was laid on and soon the speed could not be less than from 35 to 40 miles in the hour . . .
>
> [On the return journey] a most delightful line of country was presented. The view from the viaduct over the Weaver is beautiful. The viaduct consists of 20 arches and when viewed from the coach road to Northwich calls for the admiration of all beholders. From Hartford Bridge the road descends and at the end of the cutting, Vale Royal, one of the prettiest valleys in England, suddenly bursts on the eye . . .
>
> The train reached Crewe at 3 minutes to 9 o'clock. There an extra engine may assist in propelling the train up the Madeley inclined plane, but this day it was ascended with great facility. The descent from Whitmore was performed with astonishing velocity, so much so as to render writing this account an exceedingly toilsome duty. . . .
>
> At Wolverhampton, after taking in coke and water, the train again started. . . . Soon we entered a deep cutting, the banks on both sides covered with spectators. The whole of the way was crowded by the labourers [the navvies who built the line] who displayed various flags and loudly cheered the train upon its passing. The shrill and peculiar whistle of the engine gave full and satisfactory warning to the populace.
>
> . . . From Wolverhampton to Birmingham a general holiday appeared to be observed. Tents were pitched in several fields and parties given by the tenants

in honour of the day. The weather was beautiful, and the freedom from dust which exists on railways is another interesting feature connected with that branch of mechanics. . . . At half past 11 o clock the train arrived at its destination, safe, and without an accident.

This was the year when Queen Victoria, just turned eighteen, had come to the throne. It would not be long before she travelled by train herself to make rail travel, by her royal approval, into a mode of transport considered safe, sensible and respectable. But before giving her blessing to the new age, she honoured the passing of the old one when she conferred a knighthood on Marc Brunel.

By June 1841 the tunnel was ready for the ceremonial opening. On this occasion the effusive *Times* reporter had some reservations to express:

At four o'clock the sound of a gun announced that the ceremony had begun. The procession started by the shaft at Rotherhithe, led down the stairs by a band of the Fusilier Guards playing 'See the conquering hero comes'. Behind came officers of the company bearing banners, the chairman, chief engineer and an immense number of persons including ladies.

Most of the visitors went the whole distance, but looking about with an air of suspicion. Some dared not venture into the tunnel at all but remained on the staircase. Even amongst the majority there was perceptible anxiety and

Marc Brunel acknowledges the cheers from the crowd at the ceremonial opening of his Thames tunnel.

notwithstanding the singular reverberation of the music, the brilliance of the lights and all the means taken to give éclat to the event, it was evident there was a lurking, chilling fear in the breast of many; and it cannot be denied that the very walls were dripping in a cold sweat.

In so confined a space, the accumulation of breaths from the crowd, the dampness of the ground and the flaring upwards of 130 gaslights, combined to create an atmosphere disgustingly heated and fetid. So it was with much puffing that the procession emerged once again from the shaft, uttering in expressive ejaculations their delight at once more beholding the light of heaven and breathing pure air.

But given the many difficulties overcome, the vast sums of money spent, including £280,000 from the public purse, and despite the melancholy fact that many lives have been lost, one is compelled to agree with a wheezy citizen who declared – 'Well, it is a wonderful undertaking.' Some exquisite medals to commemorate the event were sold among the visitors while at the tunnel pier the watermen hoisted a black flag – to indicate what *they* felt about the tunnel that had undermined their interests.

The watermen were soon to discover that the tunnel did not threaten their livelihood at all. Marc had long since designed what he liked to call the Great Descents – the approach roads that in vast circles on each bank would spiral down to the tunnel below. But no one had yet bought the land required for them; and there was now no money left to build them anyway.

When Marc and Isambard had laid the first bricks of the Rotherhithe shaft back in 1825, it was confidently predicted that the wine to be drunk the other side on completion of the work would have only three years at most to age; and that the tunnel would have been built for not more than £150,000. Seventeen years later when the bottles at last were opened, the cost was known to be over £400,000. Yet no one would invest the relatively little now needed to give the tunnel the chance to do what it was designed for and bring in some return for the vast sums spent on it.

Before it was even finished, Marc had had a second stroke. But at the ceremonial opening the little dumpy engineer had had no problem marching, albeit with his stick, proudly behind the band through the archways of his great work. The adrenalin alone kept him going. But at seventy-four he began to age fast when he realised that the company could not even meet the terms of his contract and find the £5,000 due to him for completing the work.

Isambard, now seriously rich, bought a house for his parents in Westminster and when Marc died, at the age of eighty, brought his widowed mother into his own home on Duke Street. She lived another five years, during which time she never went out except onto her balcony to look at the park. She still treasured not only the keepsakes of her life with Marc, but a jug once given her by a nun when they were imprisoned together in France under the shadow of the guillotine.

Did she ever wonder in her last years, when her son's multifarious engineering feats had made him far more famous than his father, what her husband might have achieved if the tunnel had not so utterly absorbed him? Had he finished it as soon as he hoped to, there might not have been such difficulty in finding money for the approaches. The coach trade was flourishing, and to bring the busy Dover road into the City via the tunnel would have considerably shortened it. But by 1842 horse-drawn traffic was on the way out. Investors saw a better return for their money in railways than roads. They were more interested in Isambard's work than in his father's.

Even before Marc died, the tunnel had become just a hugely popular tourist attraction – used mainly as a streetmarket by day, and at night as somewhere under cover for down-and-outs and as a resort for prostitutes.

CHAPTER THIRTEEN
End of an Era

In the 1830s a hardened farm labourer would have been regarded as a softie by a coal miner or iron worker. But neither of these was any match for a navvy. As makers of the embankments, cuttings and tunnels that our railways still depend on today, the men whose muscle power actually created them deserve at least as much respect as the engineers who designed them.

Without an inexhaustible supply of cheap labour the engineers' grand projects would not even have been thought of. Robert Stevenson would never have dreamt of building a lighthouse on Bell Rock if he had not known he could draw on a labour force that would work as hard as he demanded, and at his price, for as long as he needed it. Marc Brunel was equally complacent about the labour he relied on for his tunnel. If they went on strike – and more than once they did – he simply dismissed them and hired others. And these were men with skills – miners, masons, bricklayers, joiners. If such could be so exploited, how much more so the mere labourers that the railway builders relied on? Yet these navvies worked harder than any manual workers either before or since.

Some were country lads unable to find employment on the land or even in the cities; others were ex-soldiers, on the scrap heap after the end of the Napoleonic wars; many were emigrants from destitute Ireland. But unlike other casual labourers, they could always find work if they were willing, as they were, to tramp about the country from one engineering site to another, whether for road, railway or canal.

They necessarily lived on the job, however wild and inhospitable the terrain. In tents or rough wooden huts they are said to have shared among each other any women who joined them, and to maintain the strength they were so proud of demanded at least two pounds of beef per man per day, with quantities of beer to wash it down. Insisting they could not be expected to work hard without beer, they put away so much that many were often in no condition to work at all.

Whether they were really as outrageous as the popular caricatures that have lived on depicted them is doubtful. When Robert Stephenson's London–

Birmingham railway was held up by tunnelling problems on Kilsby Hill, his 1,250 unemployed navvies are reputed to have swarmed into local villages for such drunken orgies they soon became literally at war with the inhabitants. One of Stephenson's engineers maintained that 'possessed of daring recklessness, they act in concert and put at defiance any local constabulary, and woe befall any woman with the slightest degree of modesty whose ears they can assail by the brutality of their language.' With such a reputation they could be blamed for anything, like all itinerants. Many a fight broke out that had been deliberately provoked by local lads knowing who would be held responsible for the mayhem.

To supply their food and drink, they depended on what were called the tommy-trucks that visited the sites. Having a captive market, these mobile suppliers could charge whatever they liked. Some were actually owned by the contractors who thus got back from the men they employed every penny they laid out in wages. Some made more from their tommy-shops than they did from the engineering contracts, which made them so slapdash on the London–Birmingham that Stephenson had to fire them and take on their work himself.

Since they first appeared on the rural scene when digging the canals that had given them the name of 'navigators', they had begun to copy what each other wore till it became a kind of uniform – a white felt hat, a brightly coloured neck scarf, moleskin breeches tied at the knee, and high-laced boots. Forming themselves into small gangs, they were paid on piece work – so if one man did not pull his weight it was the others who sent him packing. They worked so hard that often they'd worn themselves out by the time they were forty; few of them lived much longer.

They were not just immensely strong, each quite capable of throwing 20 tons of soil into a wagon every day, but seemingly quite fearless too. When earth taken from a cutting was to be used to form an embankment leading to it, a railway was laid down on which stood a wagon into which the navvies shovelled the spoil they were digging. As described by an eyewitness, 'when the wagon was filled, it was attached to a horse that was then made to trot, and finally gallop, till on nearing the end of the bank it was suddenly set free and trained to step aside; so that the wagon ran on by its own impetus and, coming up against a sleeper laid across the rails, shot out the earth into the proper place for it. This process is of such skill and daring that anyone seeing it lingers on to watch with growing satisfaction.'

More dangerous still, as the same writer observed, was the excavation of cuttings by having horses at the top from each of which a rope came down over a pulley to a navvy below. Before him, leaning against the side of the chasm like a ladder, there was a steep wooden walkway. After attaching the rope from the horse up above to his barrow containing the spoil, the navvy 'takes firm hold of the handles as both barrow and man are drawn up the steeply sloping planks, the latter having his body nearly horizontal during the ascent. Should the rope break or horse stop, he is precipitated to the bottom in an instant. Yet each will do this up to twenty times in one work shift.'

They were so careless of life and limb that during the tunnelling operations on Kilsby Hill it's said that one of them, for a bet, leapt across the top of one of the shafts and dared his mates to follow. Two did and plunged straight to their deaths. But it didn't deter the next man. He also jumped – and also got killed.

Locke and his contractors, Brassey and Mackenzie, got the best possible work from their navvies by simply making sure they were never exploited and never left idle. After completing the Grand Junction so precisely to budget, Locke took over a line from London to Southampton and immediately brought in Brassey as his principal contractor. Brassey thought so highly of the navvies that when later he was asked by Locke to contract for the railway he was about to engineer in France – from Paris to Rouen, and later from there to Le Havre – he insisted on bringing his British navvies with him. Years later Locke described the scene:

> They were soon spread all over Normandy, objects of interest not only by the peculiarity of their dress but by their uncouth size, habits and manners which formed so marked a contrast with those of the peasantry. Discarding the wooden shovels and basket-sized barrows of the French, they used their own tools which none but the most expert and robust could wield. Often I heard the exclamation around them – Mon Dieu, ces Anglais, comme ils travaillent!

Not long afterwards Locke was engaged to engineer the line from Rouen to Cherbourg, a massive undertaking not completed till 1857, when Emperor Napoleon made him an Officer of the Légion d'Honneur and Queen Victoria sailed over to Cherbourg in her royal yacht to bestow on her engineer her personal approval – almost as if France was just another of her overseas dominions. By that time Locke had also built railways for the Dutch and the Spanish; Stephenson had built them in Sweden and Belgium, and Brunel in Italy. British engineers were everywhere. Britain had become the strongest industrial power on earth, the workshop of the world, and it was the engineers (and their labourers) who had largely brought that about.

*

Building embankments, by running a horse with a wagon of spoil till it was pulled aside at the last moment for the wagon to run on and tip its load over the edge.

Navvies pushing heavy laden barrows up the steep sides of cuttings, with horses above to assist them. This was the scene at the cutting made at Tring . . .

. . . which trains race through today, quite oblivious to the dangerous human toil that made their passage possible.

In the 1840s Britain had been taken over by what was called railway mania. Unlike France and Belgium in which the state ordained where railways should run, and planned them sensibly, in Britain it had been a free-for-all from the start. Now so many were running wild across the country that even George Stephenson protested. Some in the north he had been responsible for himself; others had been built by his son after he finally completed the London–Birmingham; and weaving among them were new railways built by Locke and Brassey, while in the south Isambard Brunel was not just extending many lines from his GWR but even using a different gauge for them. The battle of the gauges which followed was fought hard between Brunel and the Stephensons as their railways converged. In the end it was Brunel who had to concede, his 7 ft wide track having to be gradually relaid to conform with the Stephenson gauge that by the 1890s was being used by railways all over the world.

George Stephenson died in 1848, just a year before Marc Brunel. He had been offered a knighthood and turned it down; no way would he become one of the nobs he despised and whom he still believed despised him. He liked to make out he'd even been politely shown the door by the Institution of Civil Engineers to which his son now belonged. The fact that Robert, after his triumph with the London–Birmingham, was now generally regarded as the greater engineer of the two was not something George liked to think about.

In his last years he enjoyed telling people how watches could be mended, recalling how he used to earn money from this in his teenage colliery days. Once he visited his birthplace and went around knocking on doors just to say hello to whoever lived there. In 1845 his wife Elizabeth had died, but he had married again and bought a large mansion near Chesterfield. One day his sister, who had brought up Robert as a child, came to stay. She counted his ninety windows and observed that there were eighty-nine fewer in the house where the two of them had spent their childhood. It became his ambition to beat the Duke of Devonshire at the local flower show. He was thrilled apparently to win first prize in a competition 'open to all England' for his grapes, and he gave up a lot of his time to devising a way to grow straight cucumbers.

When he died in 1848, there were still plenty of people around who in their youth had never for a moment visualised railways, steamships or the growth of cities like Liverpool, Manchester or Birmingham. His son's near namesake was one, the Robert Stevenson who had built the Bell Rock lighthouse, still at sixty-six in good health at Baxters Place in Edinburgh. Another was Jane Trevithick, who had seen the start of it all when her late husband had run a little toy steam engine around her kitchen table. She too was still only in her sixties.

Yet by now it was a totally different world, and despite the sweated labour, overcrowded tenements, poverty, malnutrition and unemployment that the machine age had created, the end product had done so much for British prestige that it was specially celebrated at the Great Exhibition of 1851. Not that it was meant to wave the flag for Britannia. By bringing together the finest examples of contemporary art, science and industry from all over the world, it was the Prince Consort's idea to foster between nations a spirit of co-operation not conflict. The fact that most of the exhibits would turn out to be British merely reflected the state of the art.

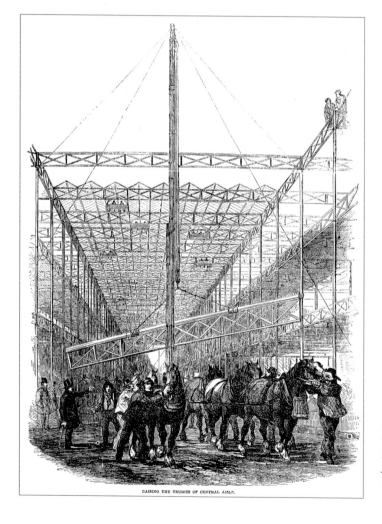

RAISING THE TRUSSES OF CENTRAL AISLE.

Raising one of the thousands of prefabricated parts for assembly into the vast Crystal Palace.

Glaziers at work on the roof of the Crystal Palace.

It was to be held in London's Hyde Park, and the first building designed for it was the product of a committee on which sat both Brunel and Robert Stephenson. It seemed to be a cross between a cathedral and a cotton mill. No one much liked it.

But it caught the attention of Joseph Paxton, estate manager for the Duke of Devonshire. He had recently grown an enormous lily which needed its own hothouse to flourish in. This had led him to design an elaborate structure of iron and glass that both protected it and showed it off. He thought something of the sort might do for the Great Exhibition, and was encouraged to put his ideas on paper. They were more than ideas, they were scale drawings of plans and elevations, albeit drawn up for him by his clerks in the estate office at Chatsworth. But when Brunel and the rest of the committee looked at them, they were not surprised to learn he was a gardener. He had designed for them a greenhouse. Only a very large one.

In fact it was so large it was to cover nineteen acres. To be made entirely of glass, wood and iron, it was beautifully proportioned, strong but airy, and soon nicknamed by *Punch* as a Crystal Palace. The committee was enthusiastic, the plans passed at once to be converted into working drawings by the engineering firm now contracted to build it. Since there'd been nothing like it before, no precedent on which to base calculations governing strength, pressure and stress in the use of iron and glass in such a big way, it's this firm not Paxton that deserves most of the credit. Paxton just hoped his building would stand up. Fox & Henderson of Smethwick had to make sure it did.

With their love of anything on a grand scale, the Victorian Londoners revelled in its sheer size: 300,000 panes of glass, 4,500 tons of ironwork, 24 miles of guttering to carry off the rain that might fall on it. Despite its size, and the complex organisation required to bring its thousands of separate parts to the site for the 2,000 workmen to assemble, it took only eighteen weeks to put up and was ready, with all the exhibits in place inside, for the Queen to open on 1 May 1851.

On display in the engineering section were steam engines, locomotives, factory machinery, and models of many great achievements from Robert Stevenson's Bell Rock lighthouse to the other Robert's latest railway bridge over the Menai. But it's the building itself that was most significant. Its strength and rigidity lay not in the walls, being merely glass, but in its structure – a skeleton framework of iron and wood that could be made to any size or height, it seemed, and reduce walls to mere coverings. It was, in fact, the prototype of all the tower blocks we know today. Bricklayers and masons no longer called the shots; engineers could now put up whole buildings in addition to making roads, railways, bridges, canals, and docks.

After the exhibition this huge edifice was efficiently dismantled, removed to south London and re-erected on the site now named after it. Had it not been for a fire in 1936, it would still be there today – not just the first major building of iron and glass, but the first to be *prefabricated*.

Brunel saw its significance. Four years later, after Florence Nightingale's constant badgering of the War Office, he designed a huge military hospital for the Crimea, in separate pre-fabricated units that merely had to be assembled on site by unskilled labour. It was all shipped out, though it arrived too late to be much use.

There now seemed nothing the engineers could not achieve. As Locke and others went on building railways all over the world, Stephenson had discovered the tremendous increase in strength that iron was capable of if constructed in tubes. His tubular Britannia bridge over the Menai was followed by Brunel's use of tubular iron for his Saltash railway bridge over the Tamar still crossed by modern trains today. If anyone believed in the limitless powers of engineers, it was Isambard Brunel.

He had long ago extended his Great Western Railway to New York, by persuading the company to finance his *Great Western* ship that crossed the Atlantic in record time and opened up the way for ocean-going liners everywhere. He followed it with the *Great Britain*, and was now about to build the biggest ship of all – and learn to his cost that even an engineer of his genius was in fact a mere mortal.

*

Rather than cut down a tree, the great transept was simply built over it.

It was nicknamed the Leviathan. 'Neither Grosvenor nor Belgrave Square could take her in,' wrote a newspaper to illustrate her size. 'She measures the width of Pall Mall and could just about steam up Portland Place with her paddles scraping the houses on each side.' To be built entirely of iron, with a double hull containing watertight compartments, it would be 200 yards long with giant paddle-wheels and a 25 ft screw-propeller powered by eight engines. With five funnels, six masts and ten anchors, it would have accommodation for 4,000 passengers and a crew of 400.

To meet the needs of the growing trade with Australia and rapid expansion of emigration there, ships like Brunel's *Great Britain* were already employed. But on the long voyage via the Cape of Good Hope they had to steam many miles out of their way to find the ports to call at for refuelling. The main point of making the new ship so large was that it could carry enough coal for the entire voyage and never have to stop or deviate at all. Engineer as he was, Brunel also knew that the bigger the ship the more momentum could be built up, making it much more economical on a long voyage than smaller ships. Having discussed the idea with John Scott Russell, a highly reputable shipbuilder who was as enthusiastic as he was, he persuaded the Eastern Steam Navigation Company to raise the vast amount of money needed, and contracted Russell to build the ship. It was an action both men would live to regret.

Russell had a shipbuilding yard at Millwall on the Thames. With the river not nearly wide enough for such a long vessel to be launched into it the normal way, he proposed building it in a specially constructed dry dock which could then be filled when the time came till the ship was afloat. Brunel thought the dock an unnecessary expense and wanted it built broadside to the river so that in a carefully controlled operation it could then be made to slide slowly and safely down into the water. Russell had his doubts about this, but recognised Brunel as the boss.

If Joseph Locke had been the engineer, Russell as the contractor would have been treated as an equal partner with all the respect his experience deserved. But typically Isambard saw him simply as a hired hand. On information received about the paddle-wheel engines, he commented that the drawings sent to him 'are like the attempts at writing of a two-year-old baby and I take credit to myself I did not resent the insult of your showing them to me.' Two months later he accused him of laziness, and shortly afterwards, exasperated by the patient and reasonable replies of Russell who always signed himself politely as 'your obedient servant', he testily answered: 'I wish you really were. I would begin by a little flogging.'

The fact is that Brunel had been constantly revising his design. He asked for certain iron plates to be thickened and at the same time extended to a greater width; and then blamed Russell for the increase in weight. He knew that the crankshaft for the paddle-wheels weighing forty tons would be the largest forging the world had ever seen, but it was hardly Russell's fault, after the three attempts made to perfect it, that it was also the world's most expensive. Brunel had achieved so much on the grand scale he could not bring himself to admit that this time he had overreached himself. The costs were soaring beyond belief, and he needed a scapegoat.

The public, of course, knew nothing of this. From the Thames they had watched with fascination a great wall of iron being erected at Millwall, little knowing that the perpetual clangour they heard from it was that of millions of rivets being closed by hand by men at work in the narrow space between the two iron hulls. Eagerly they awaited the day when the giant would somehow be eased into the water.

Soon Russell was in deep financial difficulties, owing to the many new 'additions and improvements', as he tactfully described the engineer's imperious demands, that he had been forced to make. His bank foreclosed and took over his yard. His company was liquidated, forcing the Eastern Steam Navigation Co., who had precious little money now left, to take on the work themselves.

Isambard was now fully in charge, as he always wanted to be. But he kept on Russell as shipbuilder – he knew he could not do without him – only this time he was under his direct command. With the cost already way above the total budget, he was under big pressure to get the ship launched at the earliest possible date.

When the date was announced, the excitement of Londoners was such that they flocked to Millwall that day in vast numbers in the hope, said *The Times*, of being witness to what was likely to be 'a fearful catastrophe':

Every apartment if it commanded even a glimpse of the huge vessel stretching along above the treetops was accommodating visitors. Bands were enlivening the scene at different public houses, and as the performers were already drunk by ten in the morning, miserably out of time and tune, the reader must judge what they were like at a more advanced time of day.

Brunel had already warned there would be nothing exciting to see. The ship lay on cradles that would slide slowly down a gentle incline to the water where the next high tide would lift her off. To ensure he could be heard when giving his orders, he wanted absolute silence in the yard and no one there but those involved.

But he reckoned without his directors who had privately sold 3,000 admission tickets. So instead of silence around him there was pandemonium. Nevertheless, he managed to give his first order and as hundreds of workmen began to knock away the wedges that held the cradles the crowd went quiet. 'While the noise of the hammers resounded aloft,' said *The Times*, 'even the boldest held their breath, gazing spellbound at that mass of black and bronze metal.'

For ten minutes nothing happened. There were barges lined up in the Thames from which chains extended to the hull. As they tautened under the strain, there came a sound described as 'a sullen rumbling like distant thunder' reverberating through the echoing inner chambers of the double hull. But still nothing happened – until suddenly the bows shifted, a rapid drop of several ft abruptly halted by the men on the braking drum there. Those on a similar drum by the stern were so taken aback they seem not to have been ready for the lurch at their end that followed. As *The Times* reported . . .

The heavy iron handle flew around like lightning, hurling them five or six ft into the air as if blown up by some powerful explosion. With a quiver as if she had received a heavy blow, the tremendous structure came to a halt with a heavy rumbling before the spectators had time to imagine what had occurred.

The injured men were rushed to hospital; one of them, whose body is said to have been sent flying over the crowd, soon died. Brunel had no choice but to call a halt. Later in the day he made another attempt, but to no avail. Bitterly he blamed it all on the crowd and the directors who'd admitted them: 'It was not right, it was cruel! Now I have to bear the taunts of the public.'

And taunts there were. For the next three months, Brunel tried again and again. Sometimes the hull moved as much as four inches. It was suggested by a paper called *The Statesman* that

. . . the continued adhesion of the Leviathan may prompt Mr Brunel to erect a greenhouse on the vessel, and in it plant a line of rapid growing vegetation in the hope that its strong upheaving power may finally accomplish the launch in silent majesty. Should this prove inadequate, a sufficient number of balloons may be applied to take off a portion of the weight.

It took 30,000 iron plates and 3 million rivets, all put in by hand, to build the vast double hull of the Great Eastern.

Manning the braking drum which shot five men into the air when they lost control. Four were badly injured and one killed.

Isambard, with his customary bag of cigars round his neck, against the chains of the braking drum.

Punch pictured Isambard gazing hopefully on his ship and calling out 'like another Galileo, truly she moved!' Letters poured in. One suggested getting five hundred troops to march around the deck at the double 'to the music of drum and fife so that they keep in step, and the vibration set up will be sufficient to start the ship moving down your slipways.' Another recommended calling in the artillery. 'The discharge of mortars behind each of your launch cradles will soon set them going.'

Meanwhile the company was losing a fortune. But with the aid of twenty-one hydraulic rams, specially ordered at whatever the cost, the ship was gradually inched down till at last, after three months of effort, she was on the edge of the water. On 31 January 1858, with the last of the spring tides due that morning, a gale was blowing against the side of the ship that made Isambard despair. But as the tide rose the wind changed as if to help it and blew from the east. The stern lifted; a tug from the winches raised the bows. Brunel's luck had turned. His ship was afloat.

Isambard with John Scott Russell, far left, at the abortive launch.

The launch had cost ten times the amount estimated. The company was as good as bankrupt and Brunel utterly exhausted. He had been virtually living in the yard and, though not yet knowing it, was suffering from Bright's disease. So his wife took him off to Switzerland, while his great babe, as he often called his ship, lay at her moorings in Deptford waiting to be fitted out. And no one had the money to pay for that – till eventually, more than a year after the launch, when Isambard on doctor's orders was then spending the winter in the warm climate of Egypt, he learnt that a new company which had acquired the ship for £160,000 had now accepted a tender to fit her out. It was from none other than John Scott Russell.

Before Isambard even went to Switzerland there'd been talk of approaching Russell again, and in his poor state of health he had wearily consented; at that time, with no money left in the kitty, it seemed very academic anyway. Now on his return from Egypt, feeling better for the time he had spent there, he took charge again as engineer and all the old arguments with Russell broke out once more.

Not that Russell took much notice now. Everyone seemed to regard him as the real creator of the ship, though he always pointed out that the credit must go to Brunel as engineer. But Brunel was a sick man, and with most work now having nothing to do with engineering, the army of glaziers, plumbers, joiners, decorators, upholsterers may not even have known who the testy little man was with the stick and balding head who kept poking his nose into everything and generally getting in the way. But Brunel knew by now he had only a short time to live, and having set his heart on sailing with the ship on the first leg of her maiden voyage, he had personal reasons for not wanting to delay departure unduly.

As the sailing date approached, *The Times* reporter described the grand saloons and state rooms, lavishly furnished with all the profuse decoration the Victorians loved, mahogany furniture, thick pile carpets, gilt mirrors, silk hangings, glittering chandeliers, as 'all the sights of a great hotel or a condensed town'.

The ship was to sail down the estuary and round the coast to Weymouth. The day before she left, Brunel had taken possession of his cabin and then gone on deck where his photograph was taken next to one of the funnels. A few minutes later he suddenly collapsed. He had suffered a stroke which left him paralysed. So the next morning, while he lay helpless at home, his beloved ship sailed without him.

To the usual accompaniment of bells, bands and the booming of guns, the *Great Eastern*, escorted by four tugs, sailed grandly down the river. Boats came from all directions to swarm around it and wave goodbye; on the shore at

Blackwall people cheered 'with such abandon,' said *The Times*, 'it was if they had a share as Englishmen in the strongest and handsomest ship the world had ever seen.' In the grand saloons, 'the gentlemen read periodicals and chatted while the ladies played the piano and sang. But there was one void poignantly felt by all. The head which had devised this mighty structure was lying on his pillow, sore and aching.'

After anchoring for the night at Purfleet, and again at the Nore to have her compasses adjusted, the ship got at last to sea. By late afternoon on the third day she had steamed round the coast of Kent and was approaching Hastings.

Dinner was being served, but just as the dessert appeared someone mentioned the fine view to be had of the Sussex coast and everyone at once went on deck to have a look. Which was just as well. For a minute later the saloon they'd been dining in was blown to pieces by a colossal explosion. Said *The Times*:

> The deck appeared to spring like a mine. The funnel blew right up and in the roar that followed came the awful crash of timber and iron. . . . A shower of glass, giltwork, ornaments and pieces of wood began to fall like rain.

From the engine-room stokers stumbled out onto deck who had been boiled alive; a passenger grabbed one by the hand and his skin came away like a glove. Another leapt screaming over the side to be mangled to death by the paddle-wheels. A shocked *Times* reporter wrote that 'men blown up by steam can walk about as if apparently unhurt. They had an expression of intense astonishment. One seemed quite unaware that his scalp was hanging in shreds from his head.'

It was discovered later that someone had turned a stopcock the wrong way. It controlled the flow of water to the cooling jackets round the funnel, and instead of opening it further when it got too hot, he had shut it altogether. But though the explosion totally destroyed the saloons, elsewhere on the ship not even mirrors cracked 'and in the library not a book on the shelves had even stirred.'

At home, though still partly paralysed, Brunel had rallied enough to dictate some letters while waiting to hear of his ship's triumphant arrival at Weymouth. Instead he had to be told of the latest disaster. Apparently he made no comment. In fact, he seems not to have spoken again at all, except somehow finding a way to say goodbye to each of his family in turn before later that night he died.

His great ship, meanwhile, had limped into Weymouth where an inquiry was held into the accident. At more vast expense, the necessary repair work was put in hand and six months later she lay at Southampton preparing for her first ocean voyage to America. And there her captain, who had been personally taught by Brunel how to handle this colossal ship, had just stepped into his gig one day to be taken ashore when, caught by a squall, it suddenly capsized and he was drowned.

By now the ship seemed to have such a jinx on it that she sailed for New York not with the 4,000 passengers she had room for, but with a mere thirty-eight. At least they got there comfortably enough – with a crew of 400 to wait on them – and business was better on the next two voyages. But on the fourth, the ship got caught in such a storm that she lost her rudder and both her paddles; if she had not been so strongly built she would have suffered the fate of the *Titanic*. She limped back to Ireland, but her short life as a luxurious ocean-going liner was definitely over.

By now it had been forgotten she'd been designed for the long voyage round the Cape to Australia. No one even made such voyages any more, since the Suez Canal had now opened. Not that the *Great Eastern* could sail through that anyway – she was simply too wide. She came into her own eventually as a cable-laying ship, all her cabins and saloons ripped out to make room for the transatlantic

The Grand Saloon, as portrayed by the press when the ship was fitted out.

cable. She ended her days on Merseyside, as a floating funfair. When she was finally broken up, it's said that the skeletons of two riveters were found sealed within the double hull.

In his last years Brunel had become a very close friend of Robert Stephenson. When they had been making their names as railway builders they had been

The ship's vast deck.

The Great Eastern *afloat, preparing for her maiden voyage.*

business rivals, if not enemies. But as the great engineers they both were, none appreciated each other's talents more. When Robert was about to raise the colossal iron tubes that were to form his Britannia railway bridge over the Menai Straits, Brunel's admiration for what he knew to be an engineering feat of the greatest magnitude was such that he cancelled all his engagements to go and give him all the support he could. For just the same reason so did Joseph Locke. In return Robert was equally supportive of Isambard during his vicissitudes at Millwall in the building of his ship. He helped and consoled him as much as he could. His company office had always been close to Isambard's home in Duke Street, and for the last sixteen years he had lived not far from it either.

In 1842, after his completion of the London–Birmingham, his beloved wife Fanny had died of cancer; and though she urged him in her last months to marry again, preferably a woman who could bear him children as she had never been able to do herself, he never did. As a lonely widower, his friendship with Brunel meant a lot to him. And in 1859 when Brunel died he too was a very sick man.

Joseph Locke, meanwhile, seemed to be flourishing. It was his arthritic wife Phoebe who was the invalid, now largely confined to a wheelchair. Like Robert's wife she too had not been able to give her husband children, but in their case they had adopted a baby girl, now twelve years old. They lived in style in London's Belgravia, Locke's engineering achievements having made him almost as famous as Brunel and Stephenson, and just as rich. He had also achieved his early childhood ambition and become a Member of Parliament – not for Barnsley or anywhere else in his native Yorkshire, but for the 'rotten borough' of Honiton which did not even expect him to visit them.

When Robert Stephenson died – just one month after Isambard Brunel – Locke succeeded him as President of the Institution of Civil Engineers and in his inaugural Address paid tribute to them both. Little did he guess that just one year later he would die himself – quite unexpectedly, while on holiday with friends in Scotland after a day spent shooting on the moors, taken suddenly ill in the night.

His death marked more than just the end of an era. After 1860 the environment that the three of them had done so much to bring into being was to be developed in ways that meant never again would such engineers be needed.

CHAPTER FOURTEEN

A Bridge to a New World

In September 1830 a three-year-old boy, lifted up by his father to see the first trains race by at the opening of the Liverpool–Manchester railway, could still have been alive, aged no more than seventy-six, when the Wright brothers made the first powered flight. What George Stephenson launched in 1830 was not just the first major public railway, but the idea that through some form of mechanical propulsion people would be able to do what hitherto had never even crossed their minds – travel safely and comfortably at speed across land and sea wherever they chose to go.

Until 1830 most people's horizons were limited by how far they could conveniently ride on horseback. But before that three-year-old boy had even come of age he'd have been able to take a morning train from Liverpool and be in London that night. He'd have taken it for granted that railways covered the country, and fast steamships sailed to and fro across the Atlantic. Forty years on he could even have been driving one of the first motor cars.

But it was not just in the field of mechanical propulsion that such rapid advances were made. Marc Brunel's great tunnelling shield led to developments of it which by the 1880s had driven a tunnel under the Severn over 2½ miles long, and bores for underground railways in London, with almost none of the risks that Brunel and his men had had to face beneath the Thames. Machines were increasingly taking over processes formerly done solely by hand.

If Isambard Brunel could have returned to earth a mere twenty-five years after his death, he'd have been staggered by the sight of what had followed so quickly from his own and his contemporaries' pioneer work. On the Firth of Forth he'd have seen a bridge being built he might easily have dreamt up himself – a truly grand undertaking, three giant cantilevers linking arms across the Firth to bear a railway high above the water and over a mile long. He'd have noted with approval the use of iron tubes till realising they were in fact made of steel – that alloy of iron and carbon that had just begun to be manufactured on a large scale about the time of his death. It had none of the brittleness of iron, and was in every way superior and much more economical.

As for the masonry piers on which the cantilevers stood, Brunel would first have assumed they'd been built much as his own had been for his Saltash bridge – until he learnt that the water here was 200 ft deep. Instead of caissons just being floated out, upturned and sunk for the water inside them to be pumped out, they were sealed at the top and lowered below the surface like a diving bell. Inside them, men worked with specially designed excavating tools, able to breathe through a constant supply of compressed air pumped in, and to see what they were doing by the electric light supplied to them too.

On the bridge itself he'd have seen hundreds of men working at great heights with just the same disregard for their own safety as the navvies he and Robert Stephenson had employed on railways. But they were driving in rivets not by hand – like every single one of the three million required by the hull of the *Great Eastern* – but with mechanised tools, the rivets heated in portable furnaces that were fuelled by oil supplied up pipes among the girders. On the work site at Queensferry he'd have seen these men living not in tents or mud huts like the navvies, but in purpose-built barracks with shops, medical facilities, refectories and even reading rooms provided by the company.

But it was the communications system that he and Robert Stephenson would have envied most. On their railways they each had to travel in person by horse-drawn coach over long distances to sort out problems as they arose. Here on the Forth Bridge the resident engineers could be in touch with each other, and with the contractors, suppliers and foremen of every different work gang across a mile-wide waterway, simply by speaking into something they would be fascinated to hear was called a telephone. Had anything of the sort been available when they were building their railways, what time and money they would have saved, not to mention the lessening of the stress that took such toll of their lives.

Both Brunel and Stephenson would then have recognised what a totally new world of engineering had resulted from their pioneering achievements, and might even have suspected what the British people didn't realise at all at that time – that their country's position as top dog in the world was now as good as at an end.

Gone were the days when the English navvie was so much admired he was even wanted abroad. At the time of the Forth Bridge he wasn't even needed much at home any more. It was skilled men not muscle power the contractors wanted there, and these they found they could recruit more easily from Belgium, France and Italy. And though the Forth Bridge was made of British steel, this was an

In building the Forth Bridge, cranes on the giant cantilevers hoisted steelwork from barges below to be manoeuvred into place for the riveters who worked with their machines high above the Firth in cages wrapped around the massive steel tubing.

alloy so vastly superior to mere iron that industry all over the world was now calling for it. And since it resulted from a technical process that other countries were developing more efficiently than in Britain (though it was the British with Bessemer's furnace of 1856 that can be said to have invented it), it wasn't long before most of it was being produced in America, France and Germany. When iron was all that mattered and Britain smelted more of it than the rest of the world, she enjoyed a lead over other industrial nations that with the coming of steel she now lost altogether.

Soon even the coal she produced in such prodigious quantities would not give her the advantages she had once. Another fossil fuel was now on the way and there was no reason to believe Britain had any of this at all. It was oil not coal that the internal combustion engine would depend on. Even steam as the power for factories was now under threat from developments in the uses of electricity.

Though Joseph Locke anticipated the future of engineering by regarding teamwork, good planning, labour relations and the most cost-effective use of money as just as important as design and reliable building work, even he would have been amazed by the organisation of resources deployed on the Forth Bridge. And though a hands-on engineer like Brunel could well have designed it, he could never have built it with the undramatic steady efficiency of Benjamin Baker, its designer, and William Arroll, his principal contractor.

Nevertheless, however out of place they might have seemed amid the complex engineering processes their work set in motion, it was they, without any of the machinery or scientific knowledge their successors relied on, who created the infrastructure on which everything since has been built. And most of it still survives today, not as museum pieces to commemorate a bygone age, but for the same commercial purposes it was meant for.

Today's trains going north that cross the Forth Bridge and the Tay go on along the coast to Arbroath. From them you can see on a clear day the little white pointer standing up on the horizon that is Robert Stevenson's lighthouse. Its flashes still mark the position of the dangerous submerged Bell Rock as they have ever since the building was finished. Though long since automated, its structure built all those years ago entirely by hand is still so sound it requires only a visit by helicopter twice a year to check it out.

Elsewhere in Scotland motorists drive across John Rennie's bridges giving no more thought to how and when they were built than they do to the roads across the Highlands that Telford's contractors and their thousands of labourers

A print of 1840 shows a train on Stephenson's London–Birmingham line crossing Telford's road from Holyhead at Bletchley.

The same bridge, but with its upper part widened and strengthened, still carries mainline trains today.

engineered in such hostile territory in the early 1800s. Although Telford's great roads in England have largely been replaced to meet the needs of the modern motor car that Telford himself would have anticipated if anyone had listened to him, some sections of them are still in use. Take the A5 from Betws-y-Coed to Bangor through the mountains of Snowdonia and if you manage the gradients with ease, do give some credit to the man who engineered this road for you so long ago.

It's not Telford's fault that his aqueduct at Pont Cysyllte never served the purpose it was built for. Its magnificent nineteen arches rising 127 ft over the valley of the Dee is still as sound as ever. Take a trip across it and see for yourself. And though the chains suspending his bridge across the Menai have long since been replaced by steel ones, the structure he built carries more traffic today than he could ever have envisaged. So too does Robert Stephenson's road and rail bridge over the Tyne at Newcastle and Isambard Brunel's over the Tamar at Saltash.

In Bristol hundreds of motorists daily cross Isambard's suspension bridge over the Avon gorge that he himself never saw in use at all, since only the piers had been completed by the time he died. Almost within sight of it down below at Hotwells lies his salvaged ship, the *Great Britain*, now fully renovated. Between Bristol and London today's trains travel easily through the land he surveyed with such difficulty, over embankments raised, and cuttings dug, by nothing but the strength of brawny men.

When Locke was building the Grand Junction he was stalked by an admirer called Thomas Roscoe who wrote a delightful account of everything to do with this railway. After crossing the Mersey out of Warrington, he says of the viaduct over the Weaver valley: 'Immediately below is a fair vision of rich meadows and meandering streams, a scene of stillness and peace broken only by the thundering train.' It hasn't changed. Stand in those meadows today looking up at the silent majesty of the twenty stone arches above you 60 ft apart which in Roscoe's phrase 'clasp the whole width of the valley', and the only sound even now to be heard will be that of an approaching diesel which suddenly appears on the viaduct to rattle across it in mere seconds.

All Locke's works on the Grand Junction are still in use. At Crewe there was no town at all before he came surveying, just land belonging to Lord Crewe who not only consented to the railway but to a junction here too; anticipating the trade, he even built a hotel for it that is still there today, the Crewe Arms. Within eight years a hamlet of fewer than 200 had become a town of 5,000, and by the end of the century, a city of 43,000.

Brunel's great railway bridge at Saltash today . . .

. . . and Stephenson's bridge over the Tyne at Newcastle.

The Thames tunnel in Brunel's time.

Marc Brunel's Thames tunnel came into its own eventually, used today by London's Underground.

At Wolverhampton Roscoe was pleased to notice the excellent 'waiting rooms appropriate to both the sexes', for here the train had to wait for the engine to 'take breath and draw in a supply of water through a series of leather tubes'. Then:

> the brief respite completed, the sonorous station bell and shrill steam whistle announce to the lingering passengers it is time to resume their seats; and soon the train is again at top speed, cutting the air with the velocity of an arrow while the travellers themselves, reposing as they do in their armchairs and cushioned seats, see houses, trees and green fields passing by in dizzy motion as if moving under the enchantment of some magician's wand.

This delight in the journey is unlikely to be shared by commuters in the suburban trains that run every half hour through Birmingham now over Locke's and Brassey's once rural Penkridge viaduct and the enormous semi-circular Aston viaduct of 28 arches 'rising 20 ft above the valley, whose flowing line of beauty, said Roscoe, 'bends gracefully from the massy town into the beauty and verdure of the country.' Today scrapyards, workshops and streets press right up against it, and almost all its arches have long since been filled in. But it is still in constant use.

From Birmingham to London, on Stephenson's railway, passengers may not even look up when they pass under Kilsby Hill through the 1½ mile tunnel excavated at such cost in money and lives out of the lurking quicksands, but on the approach to Euston, when they are about to get out, they usually stare at the great retaining walls either side of the track that hold back the pressure from the soft blue clay.

Down on the river neither of Rennie's bridges is still there (apart from the approach arch to his London one over Lower Thames Street) but his great docks remain, though deserted by shipping. Thomas Telford's last work, the brilliantly designed and constructed St Katharine docks, with its twin harbours and joint access, is now an attractively converted leisure resort and marina.

From here it's only a short walk along the river to Wapping from where you can take the London Underground train to Rotherhithe opposite. Walk down to the platform instead of taking the lift, and you descend the stairs of the original shaft which Marc Brunel and his party so triumphantly climbed to celebrate completion of the tunnel. On the platform below you look into its arches, and in the train travel through them – in barely a minute.

Above ground at Rotherhithe is the old engine house (now containing an interesting private museum); close by, the top of the Rotherhithe shaft, and not far off the Spread Eagle public house, now called The Mayflower, to which exhausted miners were brought for 'restoratives' after nearly being drowned.

There is nothing remaining in Rotherhithe of Richard Trevithick's tunnel work; one would not expect there to be. But many of his engines can be seen at the Science Museum which even has the little model he made that he demonstrated to his wife and friends on her kitchen table in 1801.

From that day on Jane Trevithick was to live through the whole of this story – from her husband's earliest experiments, through George Stephenson's success with the *Rocket*, the coming of railways all over the country, bridges, steamships, new industry, the Great Exhibition, the story of Brunel's *Great Eastern*, even the dawn of the age of steel. She died in 1868 at the age of ninety-six.

Chronology

1793 —— Thomas Telford is put in charge of engineering the Ellesmere Canal; two years later work begins on his Pont Cysyllte aqueduct. Britain is at war with France.

1799 —— Marc Brunel arrives in London from America, marries his teenage sweetheart, Sophia Kingdom, and patents his invention for mass-producing ships' blocks.

1800 —— Robert Stevenson urges the Northern Lighthouse Board to go ahead with his proposal to build a lighthouse on the hidden reef of Bell Rock, 11 miles out to sea.

1801 —— In Cornwall, Richard Trevithick's steam road carriage makes the first ever journey to be powered by mechanical propulsion.

1802 —— An able but illiterate colliery worker, George Stephenson, gets married and a year later has a son called Robert. John Rennie starts building the new London docks. Brunel's block-making invention is taken up by the Admiralty, so the Brunels move to Portsmouth.

1803 —— Telford's proposals for opening up the Highlands of Scotland with new roads and bridges, and for a ship canal to be built through the Great Glen, get the go-ahead from Parliament. Telford appointed to take charge.

1804 —— Trevithick's steam locomotive carries five wagonloads of iron and seventy men on nine miles of railway at Penydaren. But no one can see much future for it.

1805 —— Completion of the Pont Cysyllte aqueduct. The battle of Trafalgar.

1806 —— Birth of Isambard Brunel in Portsmouth. In London Parliament approves the Bill for the Bell Rock lighthouse; Robert Stevenson begins his preparations.

1807 —— Trevithick asked to take on job of boring a tunnel under the Thames. In Scotland Robert sails with his men to start building his lighthouse on a rock beneath the sea.

1808 —— Trevithick's tunnel is almost completed when the Thames breaks in and the whole project is abandoned. So he turns back to engines and demonstrates his railway locomotive on a circular track in Bloomsbury. But no one comes forward to invest in it.

1810 —— Marc Brunel, pioneer of assembly-line methods, has invented machinery to mass-produce boots; he gets orders to supply the army. His circular saw is much in demand too. Robert Stevenson completes the Bell Rock lighthouse. And Richard Trevithick, taken ill with typhus and heavily in debt, gets back to Cornwall where he is soon declared bankrupt

1812 —— George Stephenson becomes an enginewright with permission from his employers to work for other collieries too. Soon he is much in demand and very well paid.

1814 —— Among locomotive builders he becomes the most significant through his *Blucher*, and with William Losh is soon building others and the strong rails to bear them.

1815 —— Thomas Telford begins surveying a road from Holyhead to London. The battle of Waterloo ends the Napoleonic Wars. With no more demand for army boots, Marc Brunel is soon in deep financial trouble.

1816 —— Trevithick sets sail for South America, hoping to make a fortune from the use of his pumping engines in opening up derelict silver mines.

1819 —— Telford starts building his suspension bridge over the Menai Straits.

1821 —— Stephenson meets Edward Pease who appoints him engineer on his proposed railway from Darlington to Stockton. Brunel is imprisoned for debt. John Rennie dies.

1823/4 —— Brunel's fortunes are restored when he is asked to take on the construction of a new Thames tunnel. His son Isambard, now eighteen, is eager to help. At the same time, Robert Stephenson deserts his father and prospects in England to work for mining interests in Colombia. George now relies instead on his young apprentice, Joseph Locke.

1825 —— In March, work begins on the shaft at Rotherhithe for Brunel's tunnel under the Thames; in September, the Stockton–Darlington railway is opened to enormous enthusiasm.

1826 —— Opening of Telford's bridge over the Menai, Holyhead now linked to London by his virtually completed great new road. Work on the Thames tunnel is slow and dangerous.

1827 —— Robert Stephenson returns from America to rejoin his father building railways and locomotives, while Richard Trevithick, who made it all possible, comes home at the same time, penniless. The Thames tunnel floods, but work soon resumes.

1828 —— Isambard is nearly drowned as the tunnel floods again. Work is now abandoned. Isambard goes to Bristol and enters competition for the Clifton suspension bridge; his entry rejected by the judge, Thomas Telford, who puts up a design of his own.

1830 —— The opening of the Liverpool–Manchester railway. Plans already made to extend it to Birmingham (to be called the Grand Junction Railway), and thence to London. Young Locke is much approved of by the company directors; George Stephenson resents this.

1831 —— Isambard's design for the Clifton suspension bridge approved against Telford's.

1832 —— On the Grand Junction Railway, Locke is made responsible for one half, Stephenson the other. Three years later Locke has taken over altogether and Stephenson resigns. Robert starts work on the Birmingham–London line. Telford is experimenting with steamboats on canals, and backing the development of steam carriages for use on his roads.

1833 —— Isambard Brunel starts surveying a railway from Bristol to London. Richard Trevithick dies in Dartford to be buried in a pauper's grave.

1834 —— Thomas Telford dies in London to be buried in Westminster Abbey.

1835 —— A government grant enables the aged Marc Brunel to resume work on his Thames tunnel. His son's Great Western Railway from London to Bristol now being built; Isambard wants to extend it to New York with his ship, the *Great Western*.

1836 —— Locke completes the Grand Junction Railway ahead of schedule and within budget. Robert Stephenson faces immense constructional problems on the line to London.

1838 —— London–Birmingham railway finished at last. Locke now building one from London to Southampton. In the Midlands and north George Stephenson's operations everywhere; the railway age has dawned. At same time Brunel's *Great Western* ship beats all rivals on the transatlantic crossing. Isambard, now married, is rich and famous.

1840 —— Locke goes to France to build railways there.

1842 —— The Thames tunnel completed at last. Glory for the aged Marc Brunel. But no one has the money to build the approach roads, so it is never used.

1843–46 —— Isambard's ship, the *Great Britain*, launched – to be driven by a screw propeller. Railway mania at its height. But Brunel's tracks are on a wider gauge than the Stephensons'; bitter rivalry between them. George builds railways in Spain, Locke still in France. Robert builds a railway bridge using iron tubes for extra strength.

1848 —— George Stephenson dies.

1849 —— Marc Brunel dies.

1851 ——The Great Exhibition. Paxton's Crystal Palace opens the way for prefabricated buildings. Engineers seem all-powerful.

1854 —— Brunel designs the largest ship ever, the *Great Eastern*, to be built by John Scott Russell on the Thames. Bitter arguments between the two men.

1857/8 —— Brunel humiliated by his failure to launch the ship. But inch by inch it gets into the water eventually – to be fitted out by John Scott Russell.

1859 —— Brunel, a very sick man, has a stroke just hours before the ship begins its maiden voyage. It sails without him and suffers a major accident in the Channel. The news reaches Isambard Brunel now paralysed, and a few days later he dies.

1860 —— Robert Stephenson and Joseph Locke have now died too. It's the end of an era. By the time the Forth Bridge is being built some thirty years later, electricity is taking over from steam, steel has replaced iron and the muscle power of men has been largely superseded by machinery and technology. A new age has dawned.

Select Bibliography

Since the purpose of this book has been simply to tell the story of the pioneer engineers, chronicling the events as they happened, without holding up the narrative by dwelling at length on anyone's individual talent, it is necessarily no more than a general overview. For a deeper and more comprehensive study of the subject, readers are referred to the many biographies and other books I consulted, to all of which I am heavily indebted. These are:

Isambard Kingdom Brunel, L.T.C. Rolt (Longmans; Penguin Books, 1957)
Isambard Kingdom Brunel, Adrian Vaughan (John Murray, 1991)
The Brunels, Father and Son, Celia Noble (London, Cobden Sanderson, 1938)
Memoir of the Life of Sir Marc Brunel, Richard Beamish (Longmans, 1862)
Marc Brunel, Paul Clements (Longmans, 1970)
The Tunnel, David Lampe (George Harrap, 1963)
Brunel and His World, John Pudney (Thames and Hudson, 1974)
John Scott Russell, George Emerson (John Murray, 1977)

History of Arbroath, George Hay (1876)
The World's Lighthouses before 1820, D. Alan Stevenson (1950)
Rock Lighthouses of Great Britain, Christopher Nicholson (Patrick Stephens, 1983)
Records of a Family of Engineers, Robert Louis Stevenson (Chatto & Windus, 1912)
A Star for Seamen, Craig Mair (Murray, 1978)
Account of the Bell Rock Lighthouse, Robert Stevenson (Edinburgh, Constable, 1824)
John Rennie, a Great Engineer, C.T.G. Boucher (Manchester University Press, 1963)

The Cornish Giant, Richard Trevithick, L.T.C. Rolt (Lutterworth, 1960)
The Life of Richard Trevithick, Francis Trevithick (2 vols) (Spon, 1872)
Richard Trevithick, H.W. Dickinson and A. Titley (Cambridge University Press, 1934)

Thomas Telford, L.T.C. Rolt (Longmans, 1958; Pelican Books, 1979)
The Story of Telford, Sir Alexander Gibb (London, Alexander MacLehose, 1935)
Thomas Telford, Engineer, edited A. Penfold (Telford Ltd, 1980)
William Jessop, Charles Hadfield and A.W. Skempton (David & Charles, 1979)

George & Robert Stephenson, L.T.C. Rolt (Longmans, 1960)

George Stephenson, Hunter Davies (Weidenfeld & Nicolson, 1975)

The Life of Robert Stephenson, J.C. Jeaffreson (2 vols) (Longmans, 1864)

The North Eastern Railway, W.W. Tomlinson (London, Longmans, 1914)

Joseph Locke, Railway Revolutionary, N.W. Webster (Allen & Unwin, 1970)

The Life of Joseph Locke, Joseph Devey (Richard Bentley, 1862)

Britain's First Trunk Line, N.W. Webster (Adams & Dart, 1972)

Thomas Brassey, Railway Builder, Charles Walker (Muller, 1969)

The Life and Labours of Mr Brassey, Arthur Helps (Bell & Sons, 1872)

Guide to the Grand Junction Railway, E. and W. Osborne (1839)

Home and Country Scenes on the London–Birmingham and Grand Junction Railways, Thomas Roscoe
    (Charles Tilt, 1839)

The Forth Bridge, P. Phillips (Grant, 1899)

The Forth Bridge and Its Builders, Rolt Hammond (Eyre & Spottiswoode, 1964)

'The Forth Bridge', W. Westhofen (*Engineering Magazine*, 1890)

Our Iron Roads, F.S. Williams (Ingram, Cooke, 1852)

Personal Recollections of Engineers, F.R. Conder (Hodder & Stoughton, 1868)

Lives of the Engineers, Samuel Smiles (Murray, 1862)

Great Engineers, L.T.C. Rolt (Bell, 1962)

Victorian Engineering, L.T.C. Rolt (Penguin, 1974)

The Civil Engineers of Canals and Railways before 1850, edited by Mike Chrimes (Ashgate Publishing
    Ltd, 1997)

The Railway Navvies, Terry Coleman (Hutchinson, 1965; Penguin, 1968)

The Railway Navvy, David Brooke (David & Charles, 1983)

A Social History of Engineering, W.H.G. Armytage (Faber, 1961)

A Social History of England, Asa Briggs (Weidenfeld & Nicolson, 1983)

Index

Page numbers in italic type refer to illustrations